LEADERSHIP
— with a —
MORAL PURPOSE

TURNING YOUR
SCHOOL
INSIDE OUT

Will Ryan
Edited by Ian Gilbert

Crown House Publishing Limited
www.crownhouse.co.uk – www.chpus.com

First published by

Crown House Publishing Ltd
Crown Buildings, Bancyfelin, Carmarthen, Wales, SA33 5ND, UK
www.crownhouse.co.uk

and

Crown House Publishing Company LLC
6 Trowbridge Drive, Suite 5, Bethel, CT 06801-2858, USA
www.CHPUS.com

© Will Ryan 2008

First printed 2008. Reprinted 2008

British Library Cataloguing-in-Publication Data
A catalogue entry for this book is available
from the British Library.

ISBN 978-184590084-7

LCCN 2007938972

Printed and bound in the UK by
Gomer Press, Llandysul, Ceredigion

For my Mum.

Who used to tell me that I should write a book.

Contents

Acknowledgements

I offer my thanks to my family and many friends and colleagues who have influenced this work in some way. They include:

Daniel and Christina.

Ian Gilbert and the wonderful and inspirational associates of Independent Thinking Limited.

All at Crown House Publishing.

Judy Dobson, Simon Parton, Simon Priest, Adela Bingham, Kevin Norton, Matthew Sorby, Joanne Walker, Bronwen Watson and a range of other fabulous colleagues past and present in Rotherham's primary schools and within their School Effectiveness Service.

And especially, Jackie, with whom I share many passionate debates about primary education which can rapidly move from the profound to the ridiculous and back again.

This book seeks to do the same.

Foreword

Brave heads; lazy teachers—the way I see it, those two things are what it will take to transform education in this country.

Lazy teachers because we need professionals in the classroom who are prepared to stand back and help children learn rather than lead from the front the whole time. They are the ones who put the effort into planning and preparing for opportunities where children can lead their own learning. 'The guide from the side not the sage on the stage' as it was once put. (If you're involved in setting up a new school and you find yourself ordering a job lot of interactive white-boards then this particular revolution has obviously passed you by.)

Brave heads because we need school leaders who have the strength of mind and the sheer bloody determination to say, 'This is the way it is. This is what I know—and can prove—is right for my school so this is the way it's going to be round here. And any amount of government directives, local authority hectoring or rantings in the national—or indeed local—press will not stop me'.

After all, they need you more than you need them.*

But first, no book on leadership would be complete with out a reference to Napoleon so here goes.

It has been said that he divided his generals into four types:

1. Lazy
2. Active
3. Clever
4. Stupid

---

* According to the BBC News website in September 2006, 'Schools face increasing difficulties finding head teachers, with only 4% of teachers wanting to do the job within the next five years, a survey suggests. The General Teaching Council for England predicts that four out of 10 vacancies will be unfilled by 2011...' The GTC survey of 3,665 teaching staff also found 34% of heads wanted to retire within five years.

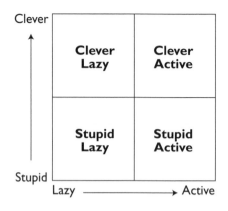

If you're reading this book as an acting headteacher think about your staff and where you would put them on active/lazy—clever/stupid spectrum (And if you're not a head maybe you could do it with family members or governors or pets ...)

As far as Napoleon was concerned the worst type of generals were the stupid-active ones. These are the sorts of people who have dumb ideas but, if that wasn't bad enough, to make matters worse, they act on them. Far better to have someone who is dumb but lazy, as they cause no harm to anyone. The clever-active ones are not ideal either as such people are always coming up with ideas you can't pooh-pooh (because they are actually quite good ideas) and then always following through on them, to the frustration and exhaustion of the rest of the troops. No, the ideal position for a trusty lieutenant, the sort of deputy you really need (and remember, a head makes things happen; a deputy makes *sure* things happen) is in the clever-lazy quadrant. Here the quality of the ideas is matched only by the desire for someone else to do the work. Or delegation as we call it these days.

Lazy teachers realise their job isn't to teach but to get kids to learn. There's a difference. 'I taught my dog to whistle.' 'Why can't it whistle then?' 'I said I taught it. I didn't say it had learned,' as the cartoon strip goes.

Shifting from teaching to learning is quite a sea change for many teachers in many schools. Developing bravery in headteachers is a different thing altogether, yet as we travel around the country working with schools and school leaders, it is becoming increasingly apparent that we need to do anything we can to encourage heads to be bold and confident.

Some of the very best headteachers I have seen—and as an anecdotal aside and one that is sure to get me into trouble, these tend to be female primary heads—are the ones saying to their staff, 'This is the way we do things. It's for the kids. If the inspector/advisor/parent/visitor/*Daily Mail* doesn't like it send them my way and I will explain.' In my eyes this is great leadership because, for one thing, it takes the pressure off the individual teacher to do what they think the observer is looking for as well as removing the fear of 'getting into trouble', a fear that seems to haunt so many staff.

So, how do you become brave? Are you born fighting the establishment or is it something you acquire out of desperation, resolution or something else that drives you?

One factor seems to be knowledge. Get the information you need to back up your hunches. Neuroscience is a great starting point. One primary head came to an INSET that I was leading at a secondary with Dr Andrew Curran, fellow Independent Thinking Ltd Associate, author of *The Little Book of Big Stuff About the Brain* and a practising paediatric neurologist at Alder Hey Children's Hospital in Liverpool. When we asked the head why he was there he said he wanted to collect 'ammunition'. He wanted to be able to stand up to the inspectors and say not, 'We do things like this because we think it's right but we do these things because we know it's right *and* here's the neuroscience to back it up.' The good thing about brain research is that, on the whole, it does back up good teaching. For example, one thing I say to reassure teachers in my INSET work is that if they are worried about having fun in the classroom when the inspectors come to call then they must remember that they are not having fun, they are (deep breath) using positive emotions to access the limbic system to optimise dopamine secretion to facilitate autonomic learning.

You could always copy that out on a bit of paper and if anyone ever criticises you for having laughter in your classrooms you can whip it out and show them where to put it.

Something else that seems to help is to have the confidence to pick and choose from the multitude of initiatives that rain down upon a head's desk on a daily basis. Each year when someone from BBC Radio 4 grabs a headteacher topping the 'most improved' league table and asks them the secret of their success, the same theme always comes through: 'I don't do all that I'm told to do.' And there seem to be many strategies for helping here from the 'if it's that important someone will chase me for not having done it' to the ingenious notion of the shelf with the bin underneath it at one end, to catch the unread files that have been added to the shelf at the other end and then worked their way along as more new files have been added.

Another thing that helps gird the loins of any headteacher when faced with the onslaught from outside is the focus of this book by Will Ryan. It's to do with knowing your overriding single moral purpose, your true north, the reason why you came into teaching in the first place. And once you know it, to hang onto it and to make it brick and flesh in the school you are helping to create.

When you work for a bank or multinational oil company or a high street retailer, no matter how far up the ladder you go, you will never be able to re-mould that organisation in your own image, to put your own identifiable stamp on it, to make it the living testimony to your own dreams and aspirations of making the world a better place. The best you can hope for is that one day you'll have your own office and in the meantime you get to choose the colour of the gonk on top of your PC.

As a school leader though, you do have a universe all of your own to shape and bend to your will. Even if you choose not to do this, you are doing it anyway, for better or for worse. But with the lives of hundreds, if not thousands, of young people in your two hands, you'd better make it for better.

Also in your two hands now is this book, a book that we hope will help you refocus on that single moral purpose that drove you into the profession all those years ago, encourage you to 'screw your courage to the sticking place' and bring the best out of your children, your staff and yourself.

Churchill once said that 'headteachers have powers with which Prime Ministers have not been invested.' That's you that is, more powerful than a prime minister. But, as Spiderman's dad once said, 'With great power comes great responsibility.'

So, be bold, be brave, be true to your vision and use it well.

Ian Gilbert
Suffolk
April 2008

Introduction

Less of a book—more of a campaign

This book shows primary school leaders how to create vision and lead their school to an outstanding future by turning their school inside out. The time is right. We must grasp the opportunity—there is no time to lose.

There are so many positive elements to primary education in the twenty-first century. Investment has been high. Results show we have the fastest improving educational system in the industrial world. Teachers are now better technically and technologically equipped than ever before. Schools are staffed by dedicated professionals who want to make a substantial difference for pupils in both the short and the long term. The vast majority of pupils come to school because they want to and because they want to succeed.

However, there are equally elements that are deeply disturbing. Unicef state that the children in our schools are amongst the unhappiest. The independent Primary Review, chaired by Robin Alexander, tells us that over-testing has had a significant detrimental effect. Social mobility remains too low. A child's life chances are determined largely by parental aspirations and where they are born. The curriculum in many of our schools remains subject and content driven and based upon a model that goes back to the nineteenth century.

These introductory notes are being written in the week that celebrates the twentieth anniversary of the Education Reform Act of 1988. Wave after wave of government initiative has followed since this time creating a primary education system dominated by compliance and fear. Schools feel compelled to implement the latest government directive and they are fearful of a fall in results, an Ofsted inspection or Local Authority intervention.

In short the pressures all come from the outside into the school. The time has come to turn the process inside out. Those who have the knowledge and understanding of a school and its community should claim autonomy and turn primary education inside out. They should lead the school to a brighter and better future through their own minds, hearts and knowledge of the community they are serving. They should use the best of the outside—

without being a government puppet. The balance of power needs to shift towards those who have the expertise, the passion, the energy and the belief to do the right thing.

The book regularly uses the term **inside out school**. So right at the start let us describe the concept. An inside out school is driven by a clear moral purpose. The school leaders are passionate and energetic people with a clear set of values. They have unwarranted optimism and believe their children can succeed. The have a clear understanding of their pupils and recognise that they have just one childhood. They also have an understanding of the community they are growing up within. From this school leaders can create a vision of what the school needs both in the long and short term. This vision is articulated and disseminated to all. Expectations are high and tolerance of underachievement is low. Adults and children know that they can improve, have a duty to improve and a duty to help improve others. The school systematically moves towards its vision through carefully devised strategic plans and appropriate systems which sometimes involves national strategy materials and frameworks. The inside out school monitors and evaluates its progress against its own personally devised measures and success criteria.

Our best schools have already done this, and many of them have leaders with maverick qualities. However this book is not about rebellion. It is about developing a vision and creating excellent schools that meet the full needs of their community in the present whilst sowing the seeds for an even brighter future.

So the book has the fundamental purpose of helping primary school leaders create a clear three-year vision of the future. I believe that this is an important and vital activity. Too often the vision for the future sits in the mind of the head teacher or other school leaders and is guessed at by others. This book argues that vision should be clear within school documentation and disseminated and articulated to all. The book provides the background and the materials to carry out the process.

There are key areas where a school must have a vision for the future and these are reflected in different chapters in the book. In short they are:

• The curriculum and teaching and learning
• Developing positive attitudes and the social and emotional aspects of learning

- Inclusion
- The professional learning community
- Leadership
- Parents as partners

Each chapter provides background information which leads to a reality check before constructing a broad three-year vision for the future. This is followed by a statement about the progress the school will make over a one-year period. The visioning process places a key emphasis on developing key systems to make the vision work and establishing targets and measures that will be key indicators of success.

The materials are tried and tested and they have helped schools to become judged as outstanding by Ofsted. They were outstanding because they provided precisely what the pupils and the community needed, and those employed there sought to genuinely inspire young lives rather than be an implementer of frameworks. In short they successfully turned their schools inside out.

The text is less of a book and more of a campaign. For thirty-three years I have lived and researched primary education, and a while ago, Ian Gilbert—who is one of Britain's most influential and inspirational speakers on educational matters—challenged me to write the book that only I could write. It incorporates all that I believe in and also a wealth of stories from my time as a teacher, head teacher, inspector and Local Authority adviser. Each chapter starts from such a story because I think that there is so much to be learned from them. This is the book that only I could have written. I hope you enjoy it and that you use it to help you lead your school from the inside out.

Chapter 1

The Inside Out School Leader

Never doubt the capacity of a small group of people to change the world.
Indeed it is the only thing that ever has.

Margaret Mead

The Prologue

If You Scratch a Good Head …
You Find a Moral Purpose

Most primary schools are extremely popular. They are served by some amazing people who do amazing things. There are head teachers who will always walk the extra mile for any child, even those who cause them the greatest heartache. There are teachers who care deeply about their class and constantly seek to inspire pupils. When Ofsted arrive positive questionnaires are returned by parents. Research shows that the primary school and the GP surgery are the most respected organisations within a locality. Confidence should be high but too often school leaders live in a world dominated by fear and compliance. Heads fear a drop in results, not meeting their targets (which are often over-inflated anyway), league tables, the call from Ofsted and a media which believes that when results improve the tests are getting easier.

As a head teacher I was once summoned to the telephone to talk to a reporter from the *Daily Mail*. I answered with trepidation, anticipating that this could only mean that they were chasing a bad news story.

'Hello,' said the reporter. 'Could you confirm that you are the head teacher of Brinsworth Manor Junior School?' My nervous voice squeaked out the words, 'Yes, I am. How can I help?' 'Well, we are chasing up a story about the Deputy Prime Minister, John Prescott, who we understand is a former pupil of the school.'

I still feared the worst and said, 'What is it that you want to know?' 'Well,' continued the reporter, 'We have heard that when he was in his final year at the school he grew rather fond of a girl in his class. However, the girl passed her 11-plus and went on to the grammar school and John Prescott failed the exam and went to the local secondary modern school. We have heard that John wrote her a love letter prior to them separating declaring undying love, and that the girl read it with a tear in her eye, corrected it and sent it back. We need to know if there is still anyone in the school who could confirm or deny that story.'

The event was nonsensical and I still don't know whether the story was true or false. However, I have no words to describe the sense of fear I felt during those moments. The *Daily Mail* does not have a reputation for being the best friend to state education in a Labour controlled authority.

This first chapter of this book speaks about the enormous outside pressures placed upon primary schools and their leaders over recent years, and how schools have felt compelled to introduce government initiatives regardless of their situation or the community they serve. Too often this led to a one-size-fits-all model. *Excellence and Enjoyment* supposedly signalled the arrival of a new golden opportunity of personalisation with its promise to take the burden off primary schools. A government minister, addressing an audience I was a member of, stated that the government should provide cash, support and silence. This terrified me. I feared the teaching profession may not be good enough to cope with the new freedom and autonomy. I shouldn't have worried. Directors of the Primary National Strategy came and went and government meddling picked up pace.

Most teachers join the profession to make a difference for the future. They are energised by a compelling moral purpose to do the right things for children. It is time to recapture that moral purpose. There is a very real world out there. Unicef reported in February 2007 that British children are the unhappiest at school, more likely to be obese, smoke, drink and have sex at a younger age. This clearly suggests that change is needed. Schools need to consider the holistic needs of their children.

Primary schools have coped with wave after wave of government initiatives since 1988. As a consequence too many schools have become organisations that have been managed rather than led. Head teachers have been managing the implementation of government initiatives rather than thinking about the specific needs of their school and community. The professional life of many of our school leaders has felt out of control. This book is about recapturing control and developing a vision of a brighter future based upon the needs of the community the school is serving. Once the vision is described, it is the job of school leaders to ensure that the journey to a better future is achieved.

This chapter will help you to reverse the trend of everything coming from the outside into your school and start the process of turning it **inside out**. There are four key steps to take:

Step 1: Take control of your professional life
Step 2: Look at the needs of your children and establish the moral purpose
Step 3: Refuse to compromise your principles
Step 4: Model human excellence

The text urges you to be brave, to do the right things for your community and to make a lasting difference for the future.

Step 1: Take control of your professional life

It is 3 a.m. and it seems as though the whole world is asleep. But you are wide awake and your mind is racing. You are thinking about Mrs Humphries who is still accusing you of picking on her daughter Amber-Louise.

You are thinking about the Local Authority inspector who watched the direst lesson on stressed vowels within word-level work. You are now firmly convinced that stressed vowels are in fact a most uncomfortable medical condition.

You are thinking about whether the layered targets within the Raising Attainment Plan within the Improving Schools Programme are going to enable you to set numeric targets based on average point scores that will help you to reach the Fischer Family Trust D predictions for the boys in the new cohort.

If you lie awake at night swimming against the tide of these thoughts, then stop and think.

Why?

Why?

Why?

Why is it that you decided to join the teaching profession or become a school leader? You are intelligent, creative and talented. Once upon a time, maybe when you were much younger, you chose this job and no other job. All the things which are now keeping you awake were not among the reasons for joining this profession. This is a profession which you should be proud to belong to—a profession that should be changing lives for the better and shaping our future. Too many of our school leaders are experiencing the sensations of **outside in school leadership**. The influences are coming from the outside, whether it is the Local Authority, Ofsted or the government. They are coming from outside and determining what happens inside your organisation. These influences could be controlling every move you make in your professional role. And now you are being kept awake by these outside forces. Don't let them drain away your energy and life blood. Stop and think:

Why?

Why?

Why?

What made you join this profession in the first place? The odds are that it was due to a moral purpose that came from deep inside you. This moral purpose formed your principles and values and was truly energising. It may have been so powerful that it made you feel as sharp as an axe. It is now time to go back inside yourself and find that moral purpose once more. Rediscover it and bring it from the inside and wear it on the outside. Stand up and be counted for what you genuinely believe.

> Once upon a time a Rabbi was asked what he thought it would be like when he reached the Kingdom of God. He replied: 'There is only one thing I know about what it will be like when I arrive at the Kingdom of God. I am not going to be asked "Why weren't you Moses?" I am going to be asked, "Were you fully you?"'

Our greatest school leaders have four great personal traits or qualities. These are interconnected. The overriding quality is passion. This in turn provides energy, self-belief and a desire to create the right bonds. However, these qualities alone will not create outstanding schools. Organisational qualities are also needed. This comes through the development of strategy, a desire to add values and have the clear capacity to communicate, articulate and disseminate information. This is reflected in the diagram below.

	Passion	
Energy	Belief	Bonding power

+

	Strategy	
Values	Collaboration	Communication

=

Performance

Personal traits

1. Passion. Great school leaders have discovered a reason, a consuming, energising, almost obsessive purpose that drives them forward. It galvanises them to become bigger, bolder people and sustains them through difficult times. **Inside out school leaders** have the passion to make a lasting difference to a school and the people it serves. They are also passionate about the way in which this will be achieved. This passion is driven by the fact that they have a love for their school and community and therefore have a burning desire to do the right thing for them. There has never been a great leader who has been devoid of passion. Outstanding schools are created by passionate leaders. It is passion that will make the head teacher rise early and stay late in order to achieve their goal. And this is a goal that is owned personally by them—and certainly not a goal of the Local Authority or central government.

2. Energy. The passion to create an outstanding school provides energy. People of excellence grab every opportunity to shape things. They have an edge to them, an impression of dynamism that gives them an air of success. Research has shown quite simply that successful people do more than their less successful counterparts. Consider every single person who impresses you and you will see a man or woman or action. The best **inside out leaders** live as if obsessed by the wondrous opportunities each day may bring and the recognition that the one thing nobody has enough of is time. Great success comes to them from the physical, intellectual and spiritual energy that allows them to make the most of what they have. Strong self-centred people use their energy wisely moving in a clear straightforward manner.

> Our doubts are traitors, and make us lose the good we oft might win by fearing to attempt. Slay your doubts and demons with good old fashioned action.
>
> William Shakespeare, *Measure for Measure*

3. Belief. Whilst great leaders have a passion for change and considerable energy they also need belief. They recognise that nothing is forced upon them and they are not simply at the mercy of government or Local Authority dictate. They pick up the gauntlet of the challenges ahead, and meet the challenges full on, valuing every experience along the way. This concept is not very scientific, but if we believe in magic we will live a magical life and if we believe that our life is constrained by narrow limits then those limits will become real. What we believe to be true about primary education and what we believe to be possible within our school will make it true and make it happen. Whilst many people are passionate about primary education too many of them have limited belief in who they are and what they can do, and therefore they seldom take the actions that could turn their dream into reality. The **inside out school leader** has absolute belief that they will succeed and will demonstrate resilient perseverance until they do. As Henry Ford said: 'Whether you think you can or whether you think you can't, you are probably right.'

In short, **inside out leaders**:

- Define the goal
- Continually visualise the successful outcome
- Act proactively and create opportunities with the right people
- Anticipate positive responses
- Are bold and imaginative in their approach to reach people and make progress
- Never entertain self-doubt
- Are excited about the inevitable success

4. Bonding power. People of excellence are inspirational. However, they also need access to inspiration themselves. Creating change can be lonely even with strong passion, loads of energy and high self-belief. People of excellence seek out like-minded people and organisations. They learn from them and build networks where ideas are shared, developed and refined. These networks provide both ongoing and fresh impetus as the school drives forward.

Organisational traits

1. Strategy. Having a passion and genuine belief will never be enough. Passion and belief can propel you towards excellence but a clear operational strategy will always be required if you are to succeed. Passion and belief may launch your spaceship but the danger is that it will start careering all over the heavens. Effective primary schools led by **inside out school leaders** are built on a clear educational vision backed by a strong strategic plan of how to achieve that vision. They create a path, a clear sense of logical progression and a plan to make the best use of the resources they have available. The purpose of this book is to create the vision.

2. Clarity of values. Values are highly significant to the **inside out school leader**. Values are specific belief systems about what is right or wrong for our lives. They are often judgements about what makes life worth living. These values become a code of conduct for all that the school does. **Inside out school leaders** consider what values they want children to have for their present and future lives and also which values they want teachers to have, demonstrate and model on a daily basis. These could include tolerance, kindness, loyalty and self-discipline. The **inside out school** states explicitly what these values are and develops programmes to ensure that they develop consistently across the schools. There are high expectations that staff in the organisation should model these values persistently and consistently, and they fully realise that values are manifested through action and not rhetoric.

3. Collaboration. Nearly all people of excellence have an extraordinary ability to create the right bonds within an organisation. They recognise that the need to connect with and develop a rapport with others is essential. They create the right collaboration for the right purpose rather than cope with historical models. School leadership can be a very lonely existence despite the fact that leaders are surrounded by people. To be successful requires developing lasting and living bonds with others; without that, any success will be shallow and short-lived. Too often schools that are deemed to be effective crumble once the head teacher moves away. This is often due to fact that too much emphasis was placed on the autonomy of the head teacher. The **inside**

out school leader works hard to create bonds that empower others within the organisation to drive the vision forward.

4. Communication. The people who are most successful in life and shape future lives are masters of communication with others—they have the capacity to communicate vision or quest. Too many school leaders have a clear vision for primary education but lack the capacity to effectively articulate it to others. Mastery of communication is what makes a great parent, artist or politician. In short, the singer and the song come together in perfect harmony.

You most likely chose to join this profession for ideological reasons. Maybe it was because you recognised that children only receive one childhood and you wanted to help make it magical. Alternatively, you wanted to ensure that pupils would get a better education than you received in the past. Maybe you were inspired by a particular teacher who ignited a passion for teaching and learning. It could also be that you were driven by social injustice.

If social injustice was the driving force then don't believe it has been eradicated. There is now clear evidence that whilst Britain has the fastest improving educational system in the industrial world, your life chances are still largely determined by where you are born.

In the twenty-first century this should not be the case. With the easy access of modern technology this should genuinely be the era when the lad in trainers from 'Bash Street School' can rise to the fore. In the modern world knowledge is power and a route out of the poverty trap. During the industrial revolution it was hard to amass wealth if you had no money to invest in the first place. In the Middle Ages the only way to join the landed aristocracy was through birthright. Today we are in the era of high speed technology and inclusive education. Every child has the opportunity to be successful. However, it too often fails to happen because of low self-esteem and low aspiration.

Inside out school leaders take a close look at the needs of their children and establish a clear moral purpose.

Step 2: Look at the needs of your children and establish the moral purpose

> The reasonable man adapts himself to the conditions that surround him. The unreasonable man adapts the surrounding conditions to himself. All progress depends on the unreasonable man.
>
> George Bernard Shaw

A few years ago I was walking through the centre of a northern town. It had recently hit the national press. William Hague, who was the then leader of the Conservative Party, had grown up in the town and during holiday times had worked for the family's soft drinks business. This was clearly thirsty work and Hague claimed that he used to go into the town centre on a Friday night and drink up to fourteen pints of beer. One resident had written to the local newspaper to say that he was going to reproduce this act that day. He would find the best real ale in the Mail Coach, get the best game of darts in the Effingham Arms and find the cheapest beers in The Rhinoceros. However, the local wag went on to say that if William Hague did come back to the town to drink his fourteen pints of beer the locals would still call him 'a bloody great Jessie'. On this particular day I was observing a young mother with a toddler in a buggy. They came to a stop outside a fish and chip shop and the mother bent over the buggy, removed the cigarette from her mouth and said to the youngster, 'I've told you, you can't have no bleeding chips. Talking to you is like talking to a brick wall.' I believe that this is a level of poverty that should not exist in the twenty-first century. I am also aware of the significant challenges this pupil will potentially bring to his school in the near future. It seems inevitable that he will arrive with low self-esteem and very little aspiration.

Let me be clear at this point that I regard high standards in literacy and numeracy as essential. This is not a text promoting low expectations. I believe that education is the only way out of the poverty trap for many of our youngsters.

However, too much of what is now taught in our schools in the name of literacy and numeracy is in the form of academic exercises which can be easily forgotten. I appear to have reached the age of 53 and still do not know what a pronoun is. This is despite regular beatings by the 'Sisters of Mercy' at the 'Roman Catholic School of Hopeless Cases'. The teaching of Latinate grammar did not engage me or stimulate me with a desire to become a better pupil.

Despite the fact that we all run at ninety miles an hour, education remains the slowest moving industry in England. Too much of the work carried out in our schools is based on a curriculum that does not meet the needs of children growing up in the modern world. Too many classrooms are sterile places where neither pupils nor teachers take risks. The Primary National Strategy was right to promote change and the development of learning experiences that were vivid and real. However, even Ofsted have told us that at this stage the impact has been limited. One in three lessons remains satisfactory and a common feature of these lessons is that teacher talk dominates. The citizen of the twenty-first century will need high standards in literacy, numeracy and ICT. However, they will also need to be creative, flexible, enterprising and have high emotional intelligence. If you want the evidence for this look at any person specification in a job advert. Too much of the curriculum within our primary schools dates back to the 1870s when compulsory education was introduced.

Overall the content of the curriculum has changed little despite the fact that growing up is an increasingly complex process. In today's world as many as one in eight children are considered to have mental health problems and one in ten children believe they are ugly. There are rising obesity rates and yet children are exposed to thousands of junk food adverts every year encouraging them to eat unhealthy food. Children are being told to take more exercise and yet there is a housing estate in the north of England with 120 signs saying 'No ball games'. In the south of England a local council rejected plans for basketball posts to be erected on a local park for fear that it would attract children. A parish council recently dealt with a complaint about a girl riding her bicycle on the pavement because it squeaked. There are increasing fears about the safety of children near roads or mixing with strangers. As a consequence they do not spend long periods of time devising their own games, building dens in the woods or making sense of the world through play. Growing up can lack adventure and too many classrooms are sterile places where teachers fear taking risks because they feel tied to frameworks or fear being different to a perceived norm. Celebrity television shows make it popular to disparage others and this has aided the anti-swot culture prevalent in secondary schools where it isn't 'cool' to achieve in school. Pupils at a local secondary school consider attendance at the homework club as social suicide.

Despite all this primary pupils have many special qualities. The absolute majority come to school because they want to. They want to please their teacher and they want them to be the best teacher in the world. Shrewd business men have already worked this out. That is why every Christmas shops are stocked with cards to 'the best teacher in the world'. Each day represents a fresh start for many primary pupils. If the previous day has been filled with problems most children will return the following day wanting to do the best for the school and the teacher, even though sometimes true success may be out of reach.

There may be clear evidence that the curriculum in our primary schools is aimed at white middle class girls. There cannot be truly equal opportunities in our schools if there are not equal outcomes. The **inside out school leader** thinks very carefully about the needs of his or her pupils prior to shaping the school and curriculum. When Tesco build a new supermarket they look at a range of socio-economic factors to ensure that the design is appropriate and to ensure they sell the right range of stock. They use postcode information and mosaic indicators to ensure that each one uniquely serves its clients. In primary education there is still too much of a sense that one-size-fits-all. Individual schools need to create a curriculum that meets the educational needs and provides holistic health for all its pupils. The system needs to celebrate diversity and absorb difference. In creating their school curriculum **inside out school leaders** ask questions like:

- What is it like where our pupils come from?
- Do they feel safe, secure, loved and are their basic needs met?
- What do they think?
- What do they care about?
- What motivates them?
- What do they know about learning?
- Can they build relationships?
- Can they deal with conflict?
- Do they have self-esteem and high aspiration?

There could easily be streets within your school's local community where the adults have no significant qualifications. Have you considered what it may be like for those children growing up there? Equally, in other areas children could be under intense and unreasonable parental pressure to succeed.

So now consider the complexities of growing up in twenty-first century Britain and the challenges of being a child in your school's locality. Why not pause and think for a while and see if you can write five statements that start from the following stem:

Education in the twenty-first century should ...

Education in the twenty-first century should ...

Education in the twenty-first century should ...

Education in the twenty-first century should ...

Education in the twenty-first century must ...

Once the **inside out school leader** is clear about what they wish to achieve they move forward purposefully to create their vision and refuse to compromise their principles.

Step 3: Refuse to compromise your principles

Teachers should see themselves as part of the proudest profession—potentially they change lives for the better. In short, they have the capacity to maintain the current inequalities that exist within our society or create a future where every child genuinely matters and all children achieve their full potential.

Education is the great engine of personal development. It is through education that the daughter of a peasant can become a doctor, that the son of a mineworker can become head of the mine, and that a child of farm workers can become president of a great nation.

Nelson Mandela

Whilst the power of teachers is tremendous, too often they simply struggle to cope with the rapid rate of government initiatives. Each initiative in its own right is valuable, but the speed deters the development of principled leadership and the creation of autonomous self-improving schools.

However, consider what we know about our best school leaders. Some are men and some are women; some are tall and some are short; some are fat and some are thin; some are democratic and some are autocratic; some are left-brained and some are right-brained; some are old and some are young. In fact, our best school leaders only have one thing in common, and that is that they are driven by a strong moral purpose that provides them with the vision to do the right things for their community, and do not compromise their principles.

Consider the **inside out leadership** skills of Martin Luther King, who began his famous speech with the words: 'I have a dream ...' and not 'I have an improvement plan with short-term objectives and measurable success criteria ...' As a school leader the first essential is that you too must have a dream and a vision that will make your community a better place. After Martin Luther King described his dream, he lived and led it from the front, he led it from the middle by standing alongside his people and he left a legacy behind him. The **inside out school leader** has a clear view of the legacy he or she will leave behind for the school's community. Despite outside pressures they remain focused and are not detracted from the process. This book is about creating your legacy.

If you are thinking a year ahead, sow a seed
If you are thinking ten years ahead plant a tree
If you are thinking a hundred years ahead, teach children.

(Chinese proverb)

If **outside in school leadership** persists it can lead to a restricted curriculum with an overemphasis on achievement in the national tests. When the then Secretary of State for Education launched the Primary National Strategy he was quoted as saying: 'As a government we stand charged with taking enjoyment out of education and enjoyment is the birthright of every child.'

The strategy also stated: 'We will try to cut the burdens on schools and encourage them and support them in being innovative. Tests, targets and tables play a vital role in helping to raise standards but we are ready to adopt and shape them to do their job better.' The words were rhetoric; very little has changed. The system is obsessed by tests.

If the children in our schools perceive that schools are simply about passing tests then it will take three generations for the impact of that theory to unwind. There is much research that tells us to reverse the current trend of **outside in** school leadership.

- 'The school is not now a learning organisation. Irregular waves of change, episodic projects, fragmentation of effort and grinding overload is the lot of most schools.' M. Fullan, *Changing Forces: Probing the Depth of Educational Reform* (1993)
- 'Somewhere along the way, in the name of educational reform, policy makers may have confused structure with purpose, measurement with accomplishment, means with ends, compliance with commitment and teaching with learning.' L. Stoll, D. Fink and L. Earl, *It's About Learning (and It's About Time)* (2003)
- 'The focus on standards, inputs and outputs, data and accountability has been relentless. I struggle to recall a piece of legislation which, even when implemented, would have increased children's enjoyment of education and made them want to come to school more.' R. Arrowsmith, 'A Right Performance', in D. Gleeson and C. Husbands (eds), *The Performing School*, (2001)

If you are still awake at 3 a.m. tossing and turning, and the problems of work are eating into you, then the odds are that you are compromising your principles. Your mind is in conflict. You will be compromising your principles because you are either doing things that you don't value or don't own. It isn't only the sleepless night that will affect you. Other physiological symptoms will strike the next day. There will be the early symptoms of stress that the pressures of work will make you ignore. These symptoms will include different breathing patterns that feel much shallower, headaches, muscle tensions that cause a stiff neck and shoulders, skin complaints and regular minor illnesses. Your fuel tank will be on empty and yet you will still be trying to run at ninety miles an hour and going nowhere. There is no reserve tank and you will be low; you will feel that you are taken for granted, angry and resentful.

When you feel these symptoms the question becomes: will it be fight or flight?

In this context fighting should not be equated to aggression. It is about having the emotional intelligence to confront the issues in front of us and do the right thing. It is possible to fight back but I believe that the only way to correct these physiological conditions is to re-centre all your actions from your own centre of gravity. The **outside in school leaders** simply struggle with the energy that is opposing them, whilst the **inside out school leader** examines the deep fundamental beliefs inside them and uses them to provide the considerable energy that can fuel fundamental change as well as contest the myriad of little fights that head teachers face on a daily basis. Regardless of circumstance they are focused and unfreakable.

> Perhaps the most indispensable tool for man in modern times is the ability to remain calm in the midst of rapid and unsettling changes. The person who will survive the present age is the one which Kipling described as the one who can keep his head while all about are losing theirs. Unfreakability refers not to man's propensity for burying his head in the sand at the sight of danger but to see the true nature of what is happening around him and to respond appropriately. This requires a mind which is clear because it is calm.
>
> W. Timothy Gallwey, *The Inner Game of Tennis* (1975)

As an educationalist with over thirty years within the profession I believe that, upon meeting a teacher and engaging them in conversation for five minutes, I can then get them to talk about their head teacher. If I am unlucky they will simply go into a diatribe about all the things they don't do, (he never takes assembly, or teaches lessons, or talks to children, in fact he is hardly ever there …). If I am moderately lucky they will talk about the things they do and do well (she always runs an after school club, she always remembers to say thank you, she teaches twice a week …). However, if I am really lucky they tell me everything their head teacher believes and values, such as the provision of wonderful first hand experiences that create a genuine sense of awe, wonder and spirituality in pupils and inspires them to want to learn.

We all know that school leaders genuinely make a difference when they:

- Focus on learning and teaching
- Generate positive relationships
- Provide clear vision and high expectations
- Provide time and opportunities for collaboration
- Distribute leadership and build teams
- Engage the community
- Evaluate and innovate
- Engage and inspire others

Too often school leadership focuses on the following shallow strategies:

- Streamlining efficiency based on a means/end analysis to reach the desired outcome as soon as possible. In order to achieve this, a simplistic model of the curriculum will be developed, probably based upon published frameworks. There will not be the time for pedagogical debate.
- Calculating numbers to ensure that everything can be quantified through rounding people into groups. The success of the organisation will be quantified in numbers; the quality of the experience is less important.
- Constantly predicting outcomes because the organisation cannot cope with surprise or shock.
- Continually controlling everything so that all targets can be reached. Constant monitoring will take place to aid this process.

Some would argue that this is an extremely effective form of leadership and schools need increased use of numeric data as indicators of performance. However, these are exactly the same principles of management as those used in fast food outlets and these establishments may not provide either a wholesome product or a healthy diet. As restaurants they lack aspiration to be the best.

Too often our school leaders have to compromise their principles. Whilst it can lead to what may seem like an easier life it often goes too far. Before long head teachers start to forget their key principles. Too many school leaders experience a lack of harmony between what is imposed on them and what they believe in. This causes sadness, frustration, resentment, bitterness and anger. To cope, these school leaders will often then attempt to modify their beliefs. However, this will only bring further trouble and will simply lead to further irritability and discontentment with the job.

When a school leader compromises their integrity it does not happen overnight. It takes place over a far longer period of time and it can have devastating effects. Let me remind you of the Parable of the Boiled Frog:

> If you throw a frog into a saucepan of boiling water it immediately senses danger and jumps to safety. However, if you put the frog into a saucepan of cold water and very gently heat the water up until it gets to a high enough temperature to boil, the frog simply gets used to the higher temperature and stays there until it is boiled to death.

The same thing effectively happens to teachers. They enter the profession driven by moral principles and then gradually get used to a centrally imposed way of thinking. They end up constantly trying to quantify what should be a qualitative experience and seeking ways to serve and please their political masters. There is a much-used phrase within educational leadership which says that we should 'measure what we value rather than value what we can measure'. The reality of the situation is that it appears that it is easier to count the bottles rather than judge the quality of the wine.

So pause, think again and assess your present reality from the past week and see how you respond to the chart below.

1. List your key educational beliefs or those things that should be non-negotiable in your school.
2. List the things that you have done in last two weeks that were absolutely important to you.

3. Now list anything you have done in the last two weeks that potentially compromises your beliefs, values or integrity.

Once you start to refuse to compromise your principles and integrity you are in a genuine position to model human excellence and start to realise your vision.

Step 4: Model human excellence

The starting point for shaping our schools should not be national frame-works but aligning our moral purpose with our aspirations for the pupils and the community in which they are growing up. When schools genuinely do this they are in a position to shape vision and create a curriculum for the future which will incorporate the appropriate parts of the national strategies. The realist within me knows that there will be occasions when you have to 'bend' your principles. We are all part of a much bigger system. If you make a positive correlation between what you value and what you practice, and instil it throughout your school, children will bound through the doors keen to learn through the vivid and real experiences that you create. They will be literate, numerate, knowledgeable, have high emotional intelligence and be creative, resourceful and enterprising. They will believe in themselves, and you will have made a difference for the future.

When you have considered all these issues, and feel ready to set a clear direction for the school based upon principled leadership, stop and consider one more thing: Our best head teachers are always high profile within their organisation. They seem to be around every corner. They model human excel-lence through the beliefs they hold, the values they espouse, their mental approach and thinking steps, and their actual behaviour including the physi-ology they adopt. Above all else they have a four-point approach to school leadership: they do what has to be done, when it has to be done, as well as it can be done, and they do it that way all the time.

If you are lying awake at night tossing and turning over the problems of your workplace, then change. Take the first steps towards being an **inside out leader**. You will have new energy driven by a moral purpose. Set a clear direction through the creation of vision and have high expectations and low tolerance of underachievement.

This section opened with the quote: 'Never doubt the capacity of a small number of individuals to change the world. Indeed it is the only thing that ever has.' This is your chance to change your school community for the better. You may also wish to consider the words of Helen Keller who said: 'The most pathetic person in the world is someone who has sight but no vision.' The way in which an **inside out school** leader sets vision will be considered throughout this book.

Chapter 2

How to Develop an Inside Out Vision

The Prologue

Judgement Day

'Ryan is a Pillock' was the twelve-inch high graffiti welcome I got on the first day of my second headship. It was sprayed menacingly across a freshly painted green door. I remember the day vividly. It was 3 January 1993 and the temperature never rose above freezing point. The inefficient school boiler coupled with Victorian high ceilings meant that it was almost as cold indoors as out. The school was emerging from the most difficult of times. The building had just undergone a significant repair programme following the widespread discovery of a dry rot infestation and a wiring system that had been condemned. A member of staff had received a prison sentence for abuse to a pupil and there had been a serious assault on a member of staff. In the period prior to my appointment the school had no substantive head or deputy head teacher. For the previous term a senior member of staff had been leading the school.

I was unnerved and even a little frightened by the graffiti. It sent a chill of fear down my spine. However, the worst part about the sprayed message was that it was so unfair. Whoever had done it had no right to judge the quality of my work before I had commenced the job, and this made my resolve harden. At the end of the day I struggled across the icy playground to my car. The frost that covered the windscreen had the word 'pillock' once again written into it. I muttered under my breath, 'It's Mr Pillock to you lot,' and went back into school and prepared my plan to change the world.

People would tell you that I had made a success of my first headship and I thought I was going into my new job with a track record of success and credibility. Clearly others thought of me as a pillock. This truly was going to be a tough job. To make the welcome complete, twenty-five windows were smashed on one evening at the end of the first week.

In fairness to those at the school there were many good and committed teachers. To mark their commitment five of them immediately offered to do dinnertime duties in order to improve lunchtime behaviour. Ninety per cent of the pupils were well behaved and trying to do well. However ten per cent of the children took up ninety per cent of the time, and their negative impact on the morale of the organisation was significant.

There were so many things that were wrong. I knew I had to write them down because a wise person told me to list everything you were unhappy about in the first week because by the end of the second week you stop noticing seventy-five per cent of them. I sat at my desk looking into space. I was no longer sure that I was capable of the challenges ahead. I was filled with self-doubt and fear. What had I let myself in for? I sat there with pencil in hand. My mind was so confused that I didn't even know where to start the list because it felt like there was so much to do. Instead of my organised left brain kicking in and simply writing a list that would provide me with key actions to address in a systematic organised way, my over-emotional creative right brain kicked in and I doodled the following words onto the giant blotting pad in front of me.

> Inward looking teachers, with a fear to let the children fly,
> So teacher talk dominates whilst the hands of the clock creep by
> Classrooms should be rich with curiosity but here worksheets dominate,
> Colouring in, filling the gaps, underlining… feel the brains stagnate,
> They get their full dull national curriculum, deplorable, forgettable
> High ceilings, poor acoustics make lessons non-understandable,
> Graffiti, vandalism to an institutionalised dirty building that creates no pride,
> Children complain of bullying and I can't stem the tide,
> Stench ridden toilets are dark holes that fill the children with fear,
> Can I really bring change, my mind pulses, the doubts are severe.
> Determination must rise and fear I must slay
> I will be the winner on judgement day.

That evening I waited and waited for the last of the staff to go home. I asked the caretaker for a spare set of keys so that I could lock up and sent him off to his bungalow to watch the early evening news. Then I picked up a notepad and a sketchbook and set off on a tour of the school.

I systematically toured the building stopping in each classroom, all thoroughfares, the hall, library and any other nook or cranny. I imagined the date was three years hence and made simple sketches or notes of what it would be like then. I also wrote down what would be happening and what kind of learning would take place. As the clock struck 10 p.m. I felt as though I had completed the task. I looked out of the school window to see a group of a dozen youths drinking cheap lager and smoking. I knew that there had been previous problems with syringes, condoms and the remnants of glue sniffing equipment. I promised myself that the outside would become secure and that it too would become part of the dream. The exercise carried on into the weekend when I entered banks, hotels and shopping malls to see what I could glean from their layout for the design of a far better learning environment and drew sketches in my book. I then met an ally from the staff of the nearby Meadowhall Shopping Centre. She went into the ladies toilet armed with a sketchbook, and I went into the gents. We both got stopped and questioned by security and then fell into the street laughing.

So there it was inside two notebooks: A blueprint for the future, my vision of what the school would look like in three years' time. I then made a list of all the ways the school would be different in one year's time. I have learned much about vision since this time and probably did the next bits wrong but I set about convincing the staff of my dream for a bright new future. This did not go well.

The trouble was we were speaking in different languages.
I spoke of suspended ceiling, soft furnishings and a school fit for purpose.
They spoke of the need to preserve the school's architectural heritage.
I spoke of creativity, discovery, creativity, awe, wonder and spirituality,
They spoke of a need for sets of textbooks, punctuation exercises and published worksheets.
I spoke of positive behaviour, rewards, praise and self-esteem
They spoke of punishments, exclusions and retribution.
I spoke of employing a psychologist to aid the process.
They said I needed one.

By this stage a new deputy head had been appointed who was a wonderful support. We were resolute. At each staff meeting that came along we went in determined to sell the dream. Each time I spoke of the new and wonderful future, I felt this metaphorical rising of hand bags which were slammed across a row of knees. The barriers to change were high. At the moment when I felt close to defeat, something wonderful happened: four of them resigned. The people leaving were relocating, retiring or had come to the end of their contract. Some of them were amongst the better teachers. However, the minute you start to bring in your own staff the more you are in control. I selected people who shared my dream and came with no baggage from the past. By September these people were in post, a suspended ceiling was placed in the hall, a new main entrance established, toilets refurbished and a new set of school rules were designed by the pupils that accentuated the positive. As a consequence of the physical changes the children sat in assembly and for the first time could hear properly what was being said.

Children stopped charging around the place and lunchtimes became a civilised delight. From here on we were going to be proactive and not reactive.

At the end of that first day of the new school year, just after I had said goodbye to the last child, my biggest antagonist came striding purposefully towards me clutching the newly circulated school improvement plan. Although I believed it had been a wonderful day I started to feel uneasy and ready to go on the defensive. This school had been a large part of her life for over twenty years and in her own way she loved it. She looked up at me and said, 'OK, you were right and I was wrong.' I was going to say something magnanimous but she moved away too quickly. By the end of the week the whole place had a different feel. A sense of pride, belief and energy was starting to run through the place. People wanted more change and they wanted it now. So I sold them my dream of high quality pupil creativity which went right across everything the school would do, and I told the staff that it was my intention to visit every class every day to check that the work matched the dream. The atmosphere was now different: the whole staff worked on developing long, medium and short-term plans. Whilst we were doing it we joked and laughed, and instead of going home with pains between my shoulder blades my sides ached from the pains of laughing.

The laughter stopped though when the letter from Ofsted arrived informing us of an imminent inspection. It doesn't matter how much that letter is expected, it still creates a sense of fear and uncertainty. I thought we would be alright. I certainly believed we were satisfactory. I believed in our approach to the creative curriculum, but would an inspection team? The results at that time were good: we had finished thirteenth in the Local Authority rankings, which was good given some of the levels of deprivation that existed. I had so many different forms of evidence to tell the story of our success. It included a photograph taken on the day of my arrival judging 'Ryan is a pillock'. A new judgement day had arrived.

The week didn't go completely without a hitch. If there is a bucket in front of me I will put my foot in it every time. I was approached by one inspector who said, 'I need to ask a question about Religious Education in the school, Mr Ryan. Would it be fair to say it is in the embryonic stage?' I perhaps foolishly replied, 'No… it's not as advanced as that.' However, possibly the biggest blunder came at the end of the weekly celebration work assembly. Each week hard working children shared their best work from the week with the full school community. All of the staff and children and a team of inspectors sat through the proceedings, which I led rather well in my opinion. At the end of the process the registered inspector asked for a quiet word. He praised the sensitivity of the children's writing, the quality of their art work and the accuracy of their mathematics. He then pointed out that this should have been an act of worship and the assembly should have concluded with a prayer, adding that he would have to include this omission in his report. I stated that I had completed the service with a prayer and that he just hadn't heard it. He asked for clarity and said, 'What exactly did you say?' I said that I had muttered under my breath, 'Thank God that's over!'

As the inspectors left the building I asked them to write a simple comment in the school visitor's book to mark their visit. The response was short. It said, 'Watch this space'. Judgement day was truly nigh.

I stumbled across the Ofsted report recently whilst clearing a filing cabinet. So what was the outcome on that judgement day? The report stated: 'The school makes outstanding provision through its rich and diverse curriculum. Continuous monitoring and evaluation of the curriculum help to promote high standards. Provision for pupils' spiritual, moral, social and cultural development is exceptionally good and pupils show a strong sense of moral and social responsibility. The school has a strong management structure led by a head teacher with a vision and a clear sense of direction. Resources are allocated according to the initiatives planned, on the principle of providing the best education the school can offer. It succeeds. The school provides exceptionally good value for money.'

The inspection report was clearly read by those in high places. Shortly after the inspection an invitation to meet the Prince of Wales at Highgrove House arrived by special delivery. Overall it was not a bad achievement for a pillock.

This chapter explores the need for all schools to have their own vision for the future and to ensure that this is disseminated and articulated to everyone. One of the key features of schools that are judged to be outstanding is a vision for the future based upon the needs of a school's community.

The text that follows describes the process and tells you how to use this book. The materials provided in the following chapters will help you to develop your vision in a simple and exciting way that can engage either the whole staff or a school leadership team. It will lead to purposeful, stimulating and inspiring conversation that will secure your vision for a bright future. It is based upon a technique called 'whole brain visioning'. This approach allows the collective, creative right brain of the organisation to work with the collective, systematic analytical left brain of the organisation to provide a truly powerful sense of direction.

An introduction to visioning

Here is a tip for you. If your horse drops dead, dismount. There is no point flogging the proverbial dead horse. It was bound to drop dead sooner or later anyway. You have spent the last seven years chasing across the prairie, not necessarily in a straight line. Every time you made your final gallop through the canyon with the target in sight they went and changed it anyway. Go on, dismount. Take a look around you. Where is it that you want to go? How do you believe you can make this community a better place in the future? Think about it carefully and then create a vision for the times ahead and then think about the best way of getting there. Don't simply order another government steed from the Department for Children, Schools and Families Intervention Livery and Stables Company and set off on the chase again. Take control. Create your own thoroughbred. If you feel constrained by the government or outside forces you will not be adding value to the organisation.

Managing constraints ≠ adding value

Let me tell you about a particular school. It nestles between the giant Corus steel plant, the KP Nut factory and the South Yorkshire Canal. It is in an area of social deprivation. It is a small school with just over a hundred pupils. Pupil mobility is high. There is an especially mobile population within the catchment area. It frequently falls below the government's floor targets. For this reason the government could call it 'hard to shift'. However, by complete contrast Ofsted call it a good school with outstanding features. The quality of teaching and learning is good and the school provides good value for money. Ofsted describe the head teacher as outstanding. In reality she is an **inside out school leader** with a clear vision for the school and its community.

The issue of creating and inspiring vision should be central to the work of school leaders. It is a key task that makes schools stand out from the rest. Sadly it has been an element of work that has been missing from many schools over the last decade. During this period too many schools have been managed rather than led. Head teachers and senior members of staff have been forced to manage wave after wave of government initiatives. Schools have felt compelled to implement the national strategies, Qualifications and Curriculum Authority schemes of work, layered targets and cope with regular audits from Ofsted and the Local Authority. However, our best school leaders stopped and redressed the balance between leadership and management, and decided to create their own destiny. These school leaders align everybody and move purposefully into a clearly described better future that has been articulated and disseminated to all. In the meantime others are constantly reacting to the next government initiative knowing that the previous one has not yet been embedded. Some schools go nowhere simply because everybody is pushing and pulling in different directions, leading to inertia. Some **outside in school leaders** have vision but these are usually based upon organisational features of the school. However, the **inside out school leader** is committed to the fundamental purpose of the school. He/she dreams and shapes the vision around their desire to change the school and its community for the better by devising a realistic and attractive future. He/she has the skill to create, articulate, disseminate and achieve their dream through four stages.

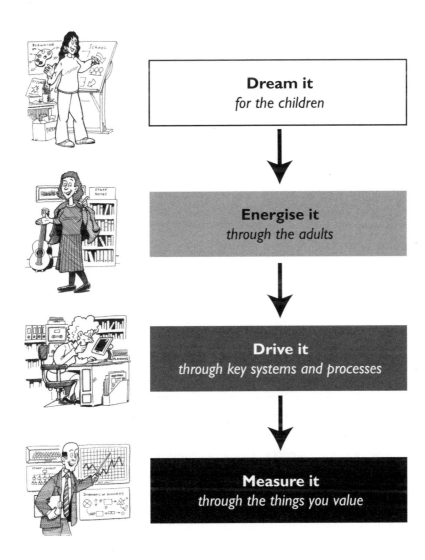

Dream it
for the children

Energise it
through the adults

Drive it
through key systems and processes

Measure it
through the things you value

Stage 1: Dream it for the children

At this stage in the visioning process the attention is entirely on the children. The **inside out school leader** develops a vision for children based upon the curriculum they will experience, the attitudes and qualities they will develop and the sensations they will feel within a fully inclusive school. There will be three parts to this area of visioning.

Firstly, the **inside out school leader** has to be imaginative and visionary. It is their desire to provide a transformational education and stimulate others into new ways of thinking. At the very centre of the **inside out school leader**'s dreams is the curriculum and teaching and learning, for this is the very core of each school's business. It is what differentiates it from any other organisation. However, this is the aspect which is often perceived as being stolen by government organisations and controlled by their agencies including the Primary National Strategy and the Qualifications and Curriculum Authority. However, the **inside out school leader** will never surrender autonomy or responsibility for the curriculum or teaching and learning. These are the areas where there must be an absolute passion to provide the right education for the children. In developing a vision for the curriculum it is essential to consider it as a source of enquiry and personal development rather than the content of knowledge. In short it must be personalised to the needs of the pupils within a school. Chapter 3 of this book will allow you to examine the current reality of your school's curriculum and devise a clear vision for the future. **Inside out schools** also place a clear emphasis on developing creative pupils who are taught by creative teachers in creative classrooms. Chapter 4 of this book will guide you through developing a vision for creativity. The school should also be absolutely clear about what the best teaching and learning environments look like. Chapter 5 will help you help you to establish a vision in this area.

Secondly, **inside out schools** are built on positive behaviour strategies and teaching programmes that build pupil self-esteem and high levels of emotional intelligence. **Inside out school** leaders recognise that a person's life chances are considerably enhanced if they have the self-confidence and the emotional strength to face the challenges ahead. They also recognise the need to develop caring, tolerant and understanding participants in a diverse society. Chapter 6 of this book will help you to develop a vision that secures positive attitudes and high self-esteem for all pupils.

Thirdly, schools need to offer a high quality education to all pupils within their care. At various stages some children will experience barriers to the learning process. This slows or halts their trajectory of progress. Schools need inclusion policies and practices that systematically identify individuals or groups who may be missing out or difficult to engage. **Inside out schools** take all practical steps to meet each pupil's needs effectively and remove barriers to the learning process. Chapter 7 allows schools to develop a vision to ensure all children are included and barriers to learning are removed.

Stage 2: Energise it through the adults

At this stage of the visioning process the emphasis changes to the adults within the organisation. The first challenge is to communicate with and then inspire the adults who will take it forward. The **inside out school leader** develops a vision of an autonomous and self-improving school which has drive and passion. They create a leadership team that influences the hearts and minds of all staff. They also work with parents so that they can play a full part in aiding their child's learning.

At the very heart of school improvement is the concept of the learning school. The **inside out school leader** places tremendous emphasis on creating a professional learning community that is passionate about teaching and learning. Debates and dialogue about pedagogy are regular and frequent. Teachers have increasingly high expectations and work hard to make lessons inspirational, vivid and real. They have access to transformational professional development opportunities. Each and every adult working within the organisation is committed to the children and it is immediately clear that the school is run for the benefit of the pupils and not the ease of the adults. Everybody believes that they can improve, that they have a duty to improve and a duty to improve others. There is a real focus on organisational learning. The learning and the development of individuals is directed by the school leaders to ensure the school is continually striving to reach its carefully articulated and disseminated vision. **Inside out schools** work to create the results they desire, where new and expansive patterns of thinking are nurtured, where collective aspiration is set free and people are continually learning how to learn together.

Chapter 8 of this book will help you to create a professional learning community where there is:

Collaboration and sharing.
Continuous teacher talk about practice.
A common focus.
A sense of efficacy.
A belief in lifelong learning.
Staff that look out as well as in.

Kath Aspinwall, Leading the Learning School (1998)

Chapter 9 will help you to improve leadership at all levels across the school. **Inside out school leaders** know exactly what they are trying to create and devise clear strategies to achieve their goals. They distribute leadership and empower others so that they can help the school reach its stated vision. Everyone is accountable for the success of the school. School leaders plan to become even better leaders. They invest in and celebrate their own leadership learning, recognising that this is an essential element in creating an outstanding school. Chapter 9 of this book will guide you through the process of establishing a vision for developing high quality leadership.

Parents can actively contribute to raising aspiration and achievement and they are often the missing link that is so frequently overlooked by schools and local authorities. Chapter 10 of this book will take you through research that will tell you just how much a child's life chances are determined by the parenting skills they experience and their commitment to education. Chapter 10 will guide schools through the process of developing the role of parents within the education process.

Stage 3: Drive it through key systems and processes

The next stage of creating a whole brain vision for your school is to consider the key systems, processes and procedures that will need to be put in place to drive the school forward in achieving the vision. I was recently talking to a newly appointed head teacher who showed me a photograph she had taken on her mobile phone. It consisted of four large, grey, loose leaf folders which contained all of the 117 policies that the school had written or adopted. They were then put back on the shelf to be forgotten about and allowed to collect dust. They would remain there until somebody arrived to check them in order that they could tick boxes. They are part of a culture of compliance and fear set up by the government, Ofsted and local authorities. A small organisation such as a primary school cannot cope with such a bureaucratic nightmare. By the time they need some of these policies they will have for-gotten about their existence.

The challenge is to reduce the policies and systems the school operates on to a working minimum. School leaders then need to ensure that the con-tent is embedded and that documentation provides a purpose and energy to the work of the school. These documents should be of the highest quality, personalised to the school and written after focussed dialogue and training within the professional learning community, because this leads to clarity of understanding.

In terms of policy statements, the following should be high profile and sub-ject to regular discussion, monitoring and review by the professional learning community:

- Teaching and learning
- Performance management
- Positive behaviour
- Parental involvement
- Special educational needs supported by an appropriate map intervention provision
- Continuing professional development
- Assessment

The school also needs to ensure that it has clear plans for the effective deliv-ery of the curriculum and a school improvement plan that is a working docu-ment that all have contributed to.

The leadership team of the school should also have clear strategies to ensure that high quality monitoring and evaluation strategies exist. This will enable them to have an accurate position of the school in terms of achieving their vision and will help them plan future improvements. The school should seek to collect information for monitoring and evaluation through a range of strategies including:

- A highly effective pupil tracking system that informs both target setting and getting, and identifies pupils for intervention programmes including those for more able pupils
- The analysis of data
- Lesson observations

- Work scrutiny
- Pupil interviews
- Parent and governor surveys
- Focused evidence trails that focus on specific aspects of the school's work using all of the above
- Analyses of school trends such as attendance and punctuality because these highlight issues relating to pupil motivation

CASE STUDY

I am aware of one primary school where they operate a half-termly system of evidence trails, which focus on a particular aspect of the school's work, to see how the vision is developing. The process lasts for a week and is led by the subject leader who is supported by a school governor. They are responsible for collecting information using all of the strategies listed above. They incorporate into the process a special work assembly where children present some of the best work being carried out within that area. At the end of the process a concise list of strengths and areas to develop is provided. This in turn leads to action plans which are incorporated into the school development plan.

Stage 4: Measure it through the things you value

The best vision statements devise a set of measures which will allow a school to monitor their effectiveness. These should be measures that relate specifically to the school and their specific needs. Whilst these may include national assessment data, they should not be based exclusively on this methodology. In short schools should measure what they value and not simply value what they can measure. It can feel like the British primary school system has become obsessed by the outcomes of SATs. The tests have become so important that in some schools they are dictating the whole curriculum and construction of the school year. Children are now inappropriately spending time practising and attending booster classes for mock tests rather than experiencing rich, vivid and focused learning opportunities. Too many children find that their final year in primary school is spoiled by the delivery of a curriculum aimed at securing a high performance in tests. As a consequence it can have little richness and leaves a poor memory in the minds of pupils as they leave the school. However, the Every Child Matters agenda has arrived. Schools have been told that they will be measured against the five outcomes of safety, health, enjoyment and achievement, economic well-being and positive contribution.

Reality shows too few primary teachers are fully aware of these outcomes. The wider perception is that schools are judged solely by SAT outcomes. Considerable pressure is put on schools by local authorities to achieve high results and the heads of senior officials in the Local Authority could roll if the test results are seen to be inadequate.

Kevin Bryant (2003) cites a school which has worked to establish all the experiences they regard as essential for pupils within their own community and then set targets in order to ensure these are achieved. They state:

> The school has only two statutory targets: the percentage of children who are to achieve level 4 in English and level 4 and above in mathematics. Whilst the targets are important they only paint part of a picture. If you don't measure what you value, what other people measure becomes valued. Therefore the following list might form the basis of what the school measures.

> Children who can swim at least 25 metres (100%)
> Children experiencing at least two residential visits (100%)
> Children achieving level 4 or above in English (X%)
> Children achieving level 3 or above in English (100%)
> Children playing a musical instrument (50%+)
> Children participating in extracurricular activities (75%+)
> Number of theatre visits from F1 to Y6 (4+)
> Children achieving level 4+ in mathematics (X %)
> Number of concerts attended from F1 to Y6 (12+)
> Amount of money raised for charity each year (£500)
> Children experiencing at least one risk taking adventure activity (100%)
> Children performing in front of an audience (100%)
> Number of performances a child takes part in from F1 to Y6 (12+)
> Children representing the school at sport (100%)
> Children achieving level 4 or above in science (X%)
> Children achieving level 3 and above in science (100%)
>
> Kevin Bryant, *Creative Use of Data: Measuring What We Value* (2003)

The above list can be a useful starting point that will help schools to ensure that children receive the memorable primary education to which they are entitled. However, it does contain gaps and there is insufficient attention given to the development of social skills, emotional intelligence and enterprise.

 CASE STUDY

A school that recently undertook this kind of visioning exercise identified targets that were similar to those above as being important to them. However they also identified the following targets:

- Ninety-five per cent of pupils will make progress within the core subjects that equates to two sub-levels (four average points) over the year.
- Ninety per cent of pupils will believe that the curriculum is both relevant and enjoyable during pupil interviews.
- More than ninety-five per cent of pupils will feel valued/worthwhile/ happy in their pupil questionnaires.
- The number of regular parent helpers will increase by fifteen over the year.
- The school will achieve Leading Aspect status for curriculum design and the Healthy Schools Award within one year.
- There will be termly access to an inspirational visitor or speaker.

This school went on to be judged as outstanding by Ofsted one year after the visioning process took place.

Stage 5: Write the vision statement

This chapter argues that there are four stages to developing a school vision statement. Stages 1 and 2 above outline the six key areas of a school's work where there needs to be a clear vision that is articulated and disseminated to all. This is reflected in the diagram below. Those parts that have a dark shade relate to the pupils within the school. Those parts that have a light shade relate to the adults. Both are highly important.

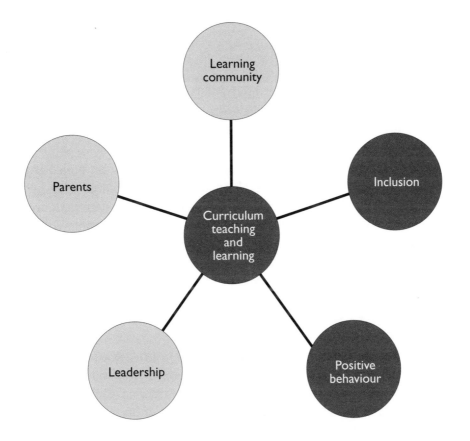

At the very centre of every vision will be the school's aspirations for the curriculum and teaching and learning. Around the circumference are the other key areas where schools need a clear vision for the future. This book will provide you with guidance prompts and professional development activities that will aid the process. Each of the chapters will commence with background information. This will be followed by an activity that will provide you with a reality check of the strengths and weaknesses of your current situation. You are then asked to paint your picture of what you would like your school to be like in three years' time. Finally, you are asked to plot your route along the journey by planning the progress you will have made within one year.

When you have a vision for the future for each of the six areas they should be collected together and edited into one single vision statement. After this has been completed schools need to develop the key systems and procedures that will drive the vision to reality by using the guidance in Stage 3 above. Finally, school leaders need to devise their own set of measures that will allow them to measure their successes as outlined in Stage 4.

The final challenge

Once the vision statement has been written and prepared, and even after it has become supported by a small number of high quality policies and documents, it is not yet complete. A final challenge remains. Your new vision statement can too easily become very forgettable. It doesn't matter how good the documentation is, in a fast moving world it can slip from the forefront of your thinking. There is also the highly dangerous fidelity factor which soon seeps into the system. As a consequence a school starts to get pulled back to old ways of working. This prevents planned systematic change from becoming embedded. The challenge is therefore to get the vision statement and key policies down to one emblem, logo or motto which is high profile within the school and is understood by staff, pupils and parents. For example, there is one school which I visit where there is a picture of a starfish in each classroom. It is accompanied by the words, 'Make a difference'. As part of this school's visioning exercise, the school had looked at the significance of an old folk tale which goes something like this:

> A man and his son were walking along the beach late one evening as the tide was going out. The beach was strewn with starfish that had been washed up by the stormy seas earlier in the day. The young boy stopped walking and, to the dismay of his father, started picking up the starfish and throwing them back into the sea. His father who was keen to keep moving said, 'Why are you doing that, son?' The young boy replied that he was returning the starfish to the sea where they belonged. The boy's father looked at him and said, 'But there are too many of them and you will never make a difference.' Whereupon the boy picked up one final starfish and tossed it into the sea and said, 'Well, I made a difference to that one.'

The emblem of the starfish in each classroom is to remind everyone that each day they should strive to make a positive difference.

CASE STUDY

The challenge of producing a simple logo, emblem or motto can be very tough. In training sessions I often begin the process by asking such questions as: If your school was an animal, which animal would you want it to be and why? If your school was a vehicle, which vehicle would you want it to be and why?

From this exercise one school came up with the emblem of a butterfly. Two members of staff backed this up with a short piece of writing that was also going to become marginally altered to become a school prayer.

> I am Treeton School,
> I am as beautiful as a painted butterfly.
> I proclaim our spirituality, the cross raised high above the school
>   for all to see.
> I embrace the children and staff, and enfold my family.
> All of my children are seen and heard.
> I care.
> I celebrate the wonder of childhood.
> My children celebrate their creativity.
> They sing like the birds in spring.
> They dance like autumn leaves blowing in the wind.
> They paint with all the shades of nature.
> They laugh and it brings on the sunshine
> My walls are invisible, our learning knows no bounds.
> I am here to guide, and nurture, and create
> The Future.

This process was the final part of the school's visioning process. The school wrote about its vision in Section 1b of the Ofsted Self-Evaluation Form and set to work on turning the vision into reality. When the school was visited by Ofsted in the summer of 2007 it was judged to be outstanding.

The best school leaders lead a school to a better and brighter future. They have a clear vision of where they are going and make sure that others do too. This is not only shared with the school community but also with others. One essential way they do this is through the Ofsted Self-Evaluation Form where schools are asked to state what is special about their school. The best **inside out school leaders** nail their colours to the mast stating unequivocally what they provide for their pupils and for the adults in the community, and they state how they will measure their success. If this is then followed by appropriate action the school will be on its way to becoming outstanding.

The process described above works because it is based upon a technique called whole brain visioning. The methodology allows you to use the creative intrapersonal and interpersonal skills of the right brain to develop the dream of a brighter future and communicate it to others. It also fully engages the logical and systematic left brain through developing key processes and measures for success.

Many have researched and written about what constitutes an effective school. I have developed the following list from a wide range of sources—at the top of the list is vision.

- Shared vision and goals
- Positive learning environments for pupils
- Pupils have rights and fulfil their responsibilities and receive positive reinforcement
- A concentration on teaching and learning that is backed by high expectations
- Monitoring and evaluating progress towards defined goals
- An organisation where staff learning is promoted and celebrated
- An organisation where professional leadership is constantly improving
- High quality home–school partnership

Our teachers sit in staffrooms day after day discussing the quality of leadership over their milky coffees. It is the way of the world. They are desperate to be part of a vision for the future. They want to hang on to your every word and take part in an exciting journey to a better future. The children look at their head teacher as he or she stands before them, willing them to be the best in the game and to provide an awesome childhood full of discovery and fun. School leaders must not let them down. They must remember: 'The most pathetic person in the world is someone with sight but no vision.'

Creating a Future
for Children

Chapter 3

Creating a Vision for the School Curriculum

Alice reached a crossroads. She asked the Cheshire cat which route
she should use. The Cheshire cat said, 'Where do you want to get to?'
'I don't know,' replied Alice. 'Then it doesn't matter which road you take,'
said the Cheshire cat.

Lewis Carroll, *Alice's Adventures in Wonderland*

The Prologue

George Alagiah, Tabloids of Stone and a Rabbit Keeping Curriculum

It was the wettest summer on record and in June huge areas of the town flooded. There was day after day of heavy rain. Helicopters filled with journalists and camera crews circled above a reservoir because there was a danger that the weight of water would cause it to burst its dam. BBC newsman George Alagiah stood in his waders, knee deep in water in what should have been streets. Two elderly ladies being interviewed by newshounds told the nation on the six o'clock news, 'You think they would have waited for us old 'uns to die before they had these floods.' And the logic of South Yorkshire baffled the country.

By the end of the day, with floodwaters rising, I arrived home exhausted after a two-hour journey. The newspaper stated that there would now be increased chances of flooding due to climate change. I read the article and turned the page. 'Children to be given happiness lessons' proclaimed the newspaper headline as I threw it down in disgust. A journalist had just produced a totally unbalanced and biased account of those schools which were recognising the genuine need to build self-belief in pupils and the necessity to actually teach positive attitudes and behaviour rather than leave it to chance. The article was clearly written by someone who felt that if our primary schools failed to teach the ancient Egyptians, society as we know it would come to an end. I think I'll have to change my daily paper.

After a long day, though, my mind was still racing and I began to ponder about the nature of the curriculum. Just exactly what did the word 'curriculum' really mean? To many people it seems to mean the content of programmes of study. Whereas in reality it should be a source of enquiry or a true, rich and vivid learning journey leading to skills, knowledge and understanding.

The day after the floods I visited an old Victorian school building close to the river. There were no children. They were still mopping up from the damage. Teams of architects and builders were assessing the structural damage whilst teachers dressed in jeans were filling skips with damaged books and resources. It was distressing to see a school in such a state. However, I saw a very old grey book in one of the skips. It was a government publication dating back to the 1930s entitled *A Handbook of Suggestions for Teachers*. It fell open at a page entitled 'The Rabbit Keeping Curriculum'. I started to read.

The Rabbit Keeping Curriculum

Rabbit keeping is easily begun and entails a relatively small outlay. There is no need for elaborate accommodation and much of the food will consist of the surplus green stuff of the garden. Of late years rabbit keeping in this country has become more important, partly because of the increased consumption of hutch bred rabbits and partly on account of the demands for pelts and angora wool. School rabbit keeping may therefore be of some influence in suggesting profitable sideline occupations for leisure and home industries for children and parents.

In the classroom good use may be made of rabbit keeping in connection with the study of biology and hygiene. The work also has undoubted possibilities on the practical side: the pupils in addition to making hutches, nest boxes, exhibition boxes and crates and boxes for the despatch of pelts and carcasses to market can take part in dressing skins, making rabbit fur garments and, if angoras are kept, hand spinning of wool.

The choice of breed will depend to some extent on personal preference. A visit to a show where rabbits are exhibited is perhaps the best way to become acquainted with the various breeds.

The initial capital should be invested in one good doe rather than several moderate ones. With careful attention rabbits increase rapidly and the provision of accommodation for young stock is generally the most difficult problem to solve. The size of the stud should be kept well within bounds, and on no account should more rabbits be kept than can be provided regularly with green food or roots.

I started to wonder. Once I had got over the shock of the idea of primary pupils being responsible for killing and skinning cuddly furry bunnies I thought of the ideals behind this curriculum. It promoted first hand experience, educational visits, creativity, cross-curricular working, enterprise education, auditory, visual and kinaesthetic opportunities, research, the use of both the left and right brain, health and safety, independence and collaboration and education that was relevant to the needs of the community rather than abstract academic exercises. The text dated back to 1935 and it was promoting curricular ideals that are still not truly embedded within primary education. External forces prevent schools taking full control of their sense of direction. At that point I wandered on, wondering if there is anything as slow as curriculum reform.

Chapter 3 argues that schools need to have a clear vision for the development of a curriculum that is personalised to the needs of pupils. The curriculum in many of our schools does not simply date back to the Education Reform Act of 1988. The subjects and the contents can be traced back to Victorian times. The time has come to ensure that the curriculum stops being the content of knowledge but becomes a source of enquiry and a journey of discovery that will equip children for both the present and the future.

This chapter also tells you to stop simply selecting the government's prescribed route through the curriculum but to select your own direction. When you know where you are going, turn on the satellite navigation system and don't deviate.

These materials will help you set the vision and select the right road.

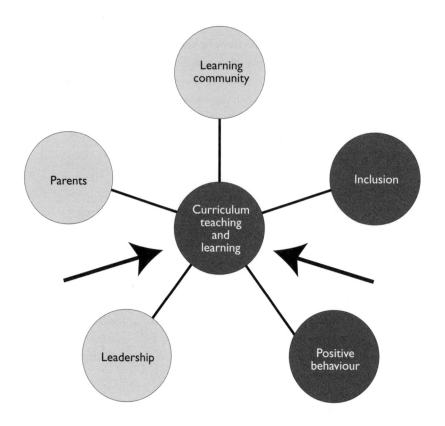

Introduction

Inside out schools recognise that teaching and learning is the core business of the school. The vehicle through which children learn is the curriculum. Therefore curriculum design should be at the forefront of school leaders' thinking. In the period prior to the Education Reform Act of 1988 many primary schools placed tremendous emphasis on curriculum design. Many school leaders produced their own unique curriculum plans based upon sound educational philosophy and the needs of their pupils. Many head teachers were ferociously proud of the curriculum they provided. Since this time head teachers believe that the powers they have had to shape the curriculum have been eroded. Dominic Wyse states:

> The period since the Education Reform Act of 1988, which first established the National Curriculum, has been a bleak time. Heavy prescription through the National Curriculum, testing, targets and league tables have resulted in an impoverished curriculum.
>
> 'Approaches to the Curriculum' in Arthur, Grainger and Wray (eds),
> *Learning to Teach in the Primary School* (2006)

Since the Education Reform Act of 1988 there has been increased government preoccupation and interference with the curriculum. The overwhelming majority of schools have felt compelled to follow a content driven curriculum to ensure that all the prescribed programmes of study are covered. Schools have passed through an era where the Qualifications and Curriculum Authority (QCA) schemes of work and national frameworks have seemed mandatory rather than recommended. Head teachers have feared that Ofsted will not be able to tick the appropriate boxes on a checklist if this one-size-fits-all model is not being followed. In their defence the government has stated that there was never an intention that all schools should follow the same curriculum. When *Excellence and Enjoyment* was published in 2003 they urged schools to claim full autonomy and shape the curriculum. However, head teachers did not trust this edict from the Primary National Strategy. This is not simply my view, but also the view of Her Majesty's Chief Inspector of Schools who identified this problem in his review of the Primary National Strategy in 2005. As a consequence most schools continued to develop a heavy programme of academic subject-specific content. This was regardless of any research into how the brain works or adequate consideration of the social, emotional or other needs of children in their locality. When I was training to be an Ofsted inspector I shadowed an inspection in an ex-mining village with high levels of social deprivation. The opening comment made by the registered inspector was, 'Thank Heavens the school uses QCA schemes of work and the children have separate exercise books for each subject.' Needless to say, I did not share the same prayer.

The government is currently reiterating its message to schools to take full ownership of the curriculum. It is part of their personalisation agenda. I believe this is because they can see the writing on the wall. Schools are fed up with following a prescribed curriculum that does not meet the needs of children in the twenty-first century. Too much of the content of the current National Curriculum lacks relevance, and children do not engage with it well enough to produce high quality work as a result of high quality learning. The government is therefore encouraging schools to personalise the curriculum to the needs of pupils. They also claim to provide finances through the Standards Fund to support this work (although the reality is that this is often targeted towards intervention programmes rather than curriculum reform). Clear messages about personalisation are also coming from QCA, the organisation responsible for the National Curriculum. Some people remain confused however as to whether personalisation is simply the latest DfES fad which will disappear sooner rather than later or a route to transforming primary education. I urge school leaders to believe that it is the latter and grasp the opportunity.

The problem is that the curriculum is seen as the content of education rather than a source of discovery and fulfilment. Too many school leaders and the readers of tabloid newspapers believe that the world will come to an end if the children do not learn about the Greeks, the Vikings and the journey of a river. We are now in the twenty-first century and the subjects taught remain the traditional ones such as geography, history and art, even though media studies, business studies or leisure and tourism may give more appropriate skills, knowledge and understanding. The subjects and content of primary education date back to a piece of legislation entitled The Revised Code published in 1862. The work of primary schools remains controlled largely by the traditional universities who seem to own the content of education. Professor Robin Alexander states:

> English primary education in 2000 is nineteenth-century elementary education modified—much modified admittedly—rather than transformed. Elementary education is at its centre of gravity. Elementary education provides its central point of reference. Elementary education is the form to which it most readily tends to regress.
>
> *Culture and Pedagogy: International Comparisons in Primary Education*
> (2000)

Middlewood, Parker and Beere argue that, 'the National Curriculum for the United Kingdom is a document that outlines what needs to be taught. An alternative approach would be a curriculum that focuses not on content, but on the skills to be developed' (*Creating a Learning School*, 2005).

The reality is that too many of our schools follow a content-led curriculum. However that may not have been the intention. The Education Act of 1988 established two broad aims that required schools to provide a balanced and broadly based curriculum that promoted the spiritual, moral, cultural, mental and physical development of pupils at the school and of society, and prepared pupils at the school for the opportunities, responsibilities and experiences of adult life.

The legislation also identified the essential skills pupils need to develop in our schools. Many of these also became lost as schools delivered the programmes of study identified in the QCA schemes of work. The key skills identified below remain important in constructing a twenty-first century curriculum:

- Communication
- Application of numbers
- Information communication technology
- Working with others
- Improving own learning and performance
- Problem solving
- Thinking skills
- Information processing skills
- Reasoning skills
- Enquiry skills
- Creative thinking skills
- Evaluation skills

Recently I listened to a lecture delivered by a visiting university professor. In his address he argued that if the energy and money that had been put into producing and analysing data had been spent on developing class-room practice, then the government's national attainment targets would have been reached three years ago. There is some sense in this argument. Data is now a massive industry but still the inspectors tell us that too many lessons are only satisfactory, teacher talk dominates and expectations are too low. There is also an argument that says analysing data makes us focus on the negative aspects of what we are poor at, and this drains the confidence away from schools and teachers.

The day after hearing these comments I visited a school with high con-textual value-added scores that had achieved its Fischer Family Trust D predictions. In short, pupil progress was phenomenal. I asked the head teacher the reasons for his success. I waited for the anticipated answer relating to high quality pupil tracking, the setting of layered targets and relating teachers' performance management targets to pupil achievement. Instead he said the success was entirely down to a focus on the key skills of the curriculum and not content, on promoting quality work and devel-oping pupil creativity. He claimed he didn't need excessive amounts of data and he gained his information from 'mooching about'. The school was an absolute delight.

The university professor also stated he had met a head teacher who had recently gone into an Ofsted inspection with no data at his fingertips and without completing the Self-Evaluation Form. The school was graded outstanding in all areas. It makes you wonder, doesn't it?

I am passionate about curriculum design. I am desperate for schools to create a curriculum where all children succeed. In the previous 135 years there is clear evidence to show that the traditional curriculum has let down masses of children. Some have even argued that this was deliberate. The Marxist view was that the education system was set up to encourage failure so that there would be a cheap workforce for the factories. This is not acceptable in the twenty-first century. Traditional industries have gone. It is also widely accepted that although high quality education is expensive, it is much cheaper than the cost of ignorance. It is essential that once and for all we create a system where there is equity and a child's life chances are not determined by where they are born. Studying dollops of prescribed curriculum content will not provide children with the skills and intelligences that they will need in the twenty-first century. The Revised Code of 1862 well and truly belongs in the past. However there is much we can learn from the past in terms of curriculum development. I would be prepared to go even further back in time to pinpoint some of my foundations of a modern curriculum. Would you?

Plato (428–348 BC)

- Dialogue between two people was the most dynamic form of teaching and learning.

- The central issue of education is to establish just and right living, and that a just person lives a life of harmony.

- A just person lives a life of harmony within a community by living a life that is appropriate to the group.

- The body is perishable but the soul is immortal. Some people have gold in their soul, others have iron and bronze.

- The challenge becomes to create those with gold in their souls. Therefore there is a need to develop their senses of a love of beauty and an understanding of order and harmony.

- Children need to be inspired by tales of great people.

- Young people need to develop a body strong enough to house their soul through rigorous physical education.

Rousseau (1712–78)

- Man was born free but is everywhere in chains.

- Takes the view that we are born good but are corrupted by society.

- The child is not a mini-adult and they have different needs to adults. Childhood should be celebrated in its own right.

- Childhood should be characterised by a life of experience rather than knowledge; and sensation rather than reason.

- Studying from books and initiation into academic discipline should occur when the child is mature enough to benefit from them. Prior to that the creation of quality experiences is what counts.

- Through this form of education children will start to appreciate right from wrong and be equipped to lead fuller lives.

The thoughts of Plato and Rousseau remain important today and are often overlooked in our overcrowded content-based curriculum. These principles would lead to children who are more emotionally and spiritually intelligent. We should never forget that your chances of success in life are eighty per cent determined by emotional intelligence and twenty per cent by IQ. Whilst in England we seem reluctant to think radically about the curriculum, the Scottish Executive Education Department has been striding purposefully forward. They recognise that different parts of the curriculum have evolved over time and when taken together they do not provide an appropriate education for the twenty-first century. They realised that the curriculum needed to be less crowded and better connected, and offer more choice and enjoyment. The curriculum proposed is a competency-based model rather than a content model. It can be summarised as follows:

The curriculum will lead to **successful learners** with • enthusiasm and motivation for learning • determination to reach high standards of achievement • openness to new thinking and ideas and able to • use literacy, communication and numeracy skills • use technology for learning • think creatively and independently • learn independently and as part of a group • make reasoned evaluations • link and apply new kinds of learning in new situations	The curriculum will lead to **confident individuals** with • self-respect • a sense of physical, mental and emotional well-being • secure values and beliefs • ambition and able to • relate to others and manage themselves • pursue a healthy and active lifestyle • be self-aware • develop and communicate their own beliefs and view of the world • live as independently as they can • assess risks and take informed decisions • achieve success in different areas of activity
The curriculum will lead to **responsible citizens** with • respect for others • commitment to anticipate responsibly in political, economic, social and cultural life and be able to • develop knowledge and understanding of the world and Scotland's place in it • understand different beliefs and cultures • make informed choices and decisions • evaluate environmental, scientific and technological issues; develop informed ethical views of complex issues	The curriculum will lead to **effective contributors** with • an enterprising attitude • resilience • self-reliance and able to • communicate in different ways and in different settings • work in partnership and in teams • take the initiative and lead • apply critical thinking in new contexts • create and develop • solve problems

The Scottish Executive Education Department is right to go back to the drawing board and start afresh with curriculum design. It is also good that they are bold enough to nail their colours to the mast whilst their English neighbours speak of excellence, enjoyment and personalisation, and then revise systems for target setting and increase the emphasis on testing. This provides very mixed messages to many schools. However, the Scottish model could be a good starting point for schools south of the border but should not be merely copied. If schools are to create a vision they need to consider clearly their priorities. Schools will have established some of their key principles whilst carrying out the work in Chapter 1 of the book. The work below will help them to consider how they will skew their curriculum by assessing the relative importance of each statement. Using the 10-point scale below, mark the relative importance of the statements.

The content of the National Curriculum programmes of study are less important to us.	1	2	3	4	5	6	7	8	9	10	The content of the National Curriculum programmes of study are very important to us.
The teaching of National Curriculum key skills is less important to us.	1	2	3	4	5	6	7	8	9	10	The teaching of National Curriculum key skills is very important to us.
Developing the brain through cognitive and thinking skills is less important to us.	1	2	3	4	5	6	7	8	9	10	Developing the brain through cognitive and thinking skills is very important to us.
The development of social and emotional skills is less important to us.	1	2	3	4	5	6	7	8	9	10	The development of social and emotional skills is very important to us.
Our pupils have a sense of awe, wonder and spirituality and this is less important to us.	1	2	3	4	5	6	7	8	9	10	Our pupils don't have a sense of awe, wonder and spirituality and this is very important to us.

This exercise is the first step in helping you to shape the balance of your curriculum. You will be in a position to apportion time by considering the balance between academic content and key skills. It will help you gauge the relative importance in your locality of teaching social and emotional skills. This idea of apportioning curriculum time according to local need is not new. In the 1990s Sir Ron Dearing carried out a review of the National Curriculum and declared that schools should have the freedom to shape twenty per cent of the curricular time around their own ideals. At that stage, I shaped a school curriculum around pupil creativity and Ofsted described it as outstanding. Another nearby school focused on developing cognitive skills in mathematics and had the same outcome.

If having read the above arguments you feel inspired and challenged to commence a new curricular journey where an emphasis on content will be replaced by a skills-based curriculum in which children are taught thinking skills and also take part in lessons which aim to make them socially and emotionally intelligent, stop for one minute ... Now assess how much of a risk you feel confident to take. This is very important. On the road ahead you must have the courage to stand by your convictions. You will need to be strong and steadfast when challenges start to emerge.

Our leadership team does not readily embrace risks in determining curriculum design.	1	2	3	4	5	6	7	8	9	10	Our leadership team will take risks to achieve a truly personalised curriculum.

Creating a vision for the primary curriculum

Creating a vision for the curriculum can lead to a total rewrite of long-term plans. Redesigning a curriculum is not a quick-fix activity. School leaders have to win the hearts and minds of the staff and pupils first and foremost. Then they need to decide on an overall philosophy for the curriculum. The final task is to settle on the intricacies of piecing the curriculum together. This process can be extremely demanding especially in small schools with mixed aged classes. However it is absolutely essential that primary schools do grasp hold of the curriculum and create the correct approach for the children in their care. The curriculum is the embodiment of everything that the school stands for. It is the vehicle by and through which the children learn. It is the root of all the school does and cannot be left to politicians and their officials. The vision and the content of the curriculum should be in the hands of the professionals working with the community they serve.

The prompts below will help you to create your broad vision for the curriculum. The left-hand column provides a series of prompts which allow you to firstly to explore your current reality. The words in bold are key phrases and I suggest you think clearly about the evidence you hold before grading your response. After completing this exercise the school should consider how significant their response is. A low score would indicate that the current situation is good. A higher score indicates concern.

Statements to help shape the curriculum	Score 1–5	Significance 1–5
Curriculum leadership 1 School leadership provides a **passionate, dynamic and imaginative lead** on the curriculum.		
Curriculum leadership 2 School leadership believes that the school should have **autonomy over the curriculum and not simply follow national frameworks and schemes of work**.		
Curriculum leadership 3 The curriculum is a **source of enquiry** rather than the content of knowledge.		
Curriculum leadership 4 The curriculum creates a **sense of aspiration** which is greater than that of the local community.		
Curriculum leadership 5 Leadership ensures that long, medium and short-term planning systems provide **teachers with energy**.		
Curriculum design 1 The curriculum takes full account of the **National Curriculum programmes of study**.		
Curriculum design 2 The curriculum takes full account of **National Curriculum key skills**.		
Curriculum design 3 The curriculum takes full account of research on **how the brain works**.		
Curriculum design 4 There are clear opportunities for the development of **thinking skills**.		
Curriculum design 5 **Pupils should be involved** in designing the curriculum.		
Curriculum design 6 The curriculum draws **appropriate links between subjects** or areas of learning.		
Curriculum design 7 There is an appropriate balance between **continuing and blocked units of work**.		
Curriculum design 8 Planning ensures **progression**.		

Statements to help shape the curriculum (*continued*)	Score 1–5	Significance 1–5
Curriculum impact 1 The curriculum makes **children want to attend school**.		
Curriculum impact 2 Pupils understand the nature of learning and **strive to become better learners**.		
Curriculum impact 3 The children are taught how to become **enterprising**.		
Curriculum impact 4 The children are taught to become **emotionally intelligent**.		
Curriculum impact 5 The curriculum helps children to become **socially responsible**.		
Curriculum impact 6 There are opportunities for **creativity in all areas of the curriculum**.		
Curriculum impact 7 The humanities and the arts are essential parts of our curriculum and **are used to raise attainment in literacy and numeracy**.		
Curriculum impact 8 The curriculum makes appropriate use of visits that create a sense of **awe and wonder**.		
Curriculum impact 9 **A range of ICT opportunities** are used as a subject and across the curriculum.		
Curriculum impact 10 The locality is used to create a **sense of identity in pupils**.		
Curriculum: Other influences 1 The organisation of the school day is **supportive of the curriculum**.		
Curriculum: Other influences 2 The school grounds and immediate locality are used to **support learning on a regular basis**.		
Curriculum: Other influences 3 The curriculum draws upon the wide range of **talents within the school community**.		
Curriculum: Other influences 4 **Classroom accommodation and learning environments** support the curriculum.		

The completion of this exercise should lead to vibrant and purposeful conversation about the curriculum. It should provide you with an assessment of your current reality coupled with a sense of direction for the future. It is now time to create a broad vision for the development of your curriculum. In the first instance describe ambitiously what the curriculum will be like in three years' time. The prompts below will be helpful. After you have completed the first part of the exercise you will be in a position to produce a clear statement that reflects your vision. This needs to be articulated and disseminated to all. It should be referred to in Section 1 of the Ofsted Self-Evaluation Form and should be a key element of your school improvement plan. The process should provide you with the internal energy to create a rich and vivid curriculum. This takes us to the next stage which is to strategically plan what will be different in one year's time. Once again the diagram below will help.

	In three years' time	In one year's time
What will be the key underlying principles of your curriculum?		
What experiences will be absolutely essential for the pupils in your school?		
What sensations would you wish pupils to experience as they pass through your school?		

CASE STUDY

One infant school in an inner city area used this checklist following a training session which arose from their discontent with the QCA schemes of work. They were concerned about pupils' low self-esteem and their capacity to take risks and be enterprising. They especially valued the development of pupil creativity. They established a vision for the curriculum based around these key features. As a consequence each class had to undertake six in depth half-termly studies over a school year. The content would be selected by the teacher who would take full responsibility for the content, skills, knowledge and understanding she sought to develop. The school leadership team was adamant that the work was not to be seen as merely consisting of academic exercises; there had to be a wider and more significant impact. As a consequence the half-termly studies involved each class in:

- Improving a part of the school or community
- Developing self-esteem or promoting the social and emotional aspects of learning
- Planning and producing something for the rest of the school community (a play, short film, newspaper, shop, café)
- Undertaking an enterprise or business project
- Basing a half term's work around a story, novel or aspect of popular culture
- Developing a sense of identity through studying an aspect of the local community

The school then considered what measures they would seek to put in place in order to judge that they had been successful in their intentions. Instead of using National Curriculum statements they worked with their local Education Action Zone and devised measures around:

- Pupil resilience
- Communication skills
- Teamwork and working with others
- Critical and creative thinking
- Problem solving
- Becoming reflective learners

Any vision of this nature needs to take account of the fact that there are actually four types of curriculum that exist in any one school. **Inside out schools** understand this and use it to secure spectacular results.

Firstly there is the *formal curriculum*. This is based on key school documentation. This would consist of the school's own long-term curricular plans which will partly have been drawn from the National Curriculum. It will include the school's personalised approach to the primary framework and any schemes of work used by the school. These will be supported by significant school policies such as teaching and learning and positive behaviour. The formal curriculum should provide clarity for all who work in the organisation, Ofsted, school improvement personnel and others about the way in which the school educates its children.

Secondly there is the *classroom curriculum*. This occurs because after the **inside out school** has drawn up its formal curriculum and established its long-term plans, each individual teacher will start to shape it in their own unique way. Each teacher will select their own style of delivery that they believe will inspire the class. They will select the rich and vivid activities the children will undertake, which stimulating resources will be used and whether the creative and original responses will be secured from pupils individually or collaboratively.

The words of the song say, 'it ain't what you do, it's the way that you do it'. This sentiment is reflected in the third type of curriculum which is often referred to as the *hidden curriculum*. Teachers in **inside out schools** have identified the immense power of the hidden curriculum. They know that if they create a positive ethos it will raise the self-esteem of pupils making them equipped to learn and want to learn. Positive aspects of the hidden curriculum include the use of praise, valuing effort and ensuring the classroom is a safe and caring place where everyone is supported and respected. Children receive positive feedback on their work from their teachers and peers and high quality work is well displayed within tidy and well-organised classrooms. However, there can also be a dark and sinister side to the hidden curriculum in some schools and classrooms. Poorly or unmarked work, loud or aggressive teachers, sarcasm and ridicule, and scruffy learning environments have a negative effect on children and they learn that the teacher does not care about them or the work of the school.

Fourthly there is an *enrichment curriculum*. **Inside out schools** think carefully about the experiences they want children to savour and the sensations they will feel during their time in school. This curriculum provides children with a range of stimulating educational visits, the chance to perform or play a musical instrument, sporting opportunities or other rich experiences that will stay with a primary school child. I believe that every primary school teacher's aim should be to be mentioned on the web pages of Friends Reunited by ex-pupils for the rich and varied activities they provide for pupils.

The purpose of this chapter is to aid you to develop your vision for the curriculum in your school. It should allow you to take the best of the government guidance but not to be dominated by **outside in** practices. Use the materials provided to carry out a whole school review and then ensure that curriculum development is staff and pupil led and owned. This will provide internal energy and build strong relationships and commitment across the school. It is essential that you consider the curriculum in a holistic sense so that there are no missed opportunities. If you can answer yes to the questions below you are probably ready to proceed with turning your curriculum vision into reality.

- Have you taken full account of how learning can be enhanced through extracurricular provision, out of hours learning and study clubs?
- Will the school use educational visits and residential experiences to enhance the learning process?
- Will the school make full use of the wide range of ICT opportunities to support the curriculum and will these be made readily available outside of lessons?
- Is the school calendar flexible enough to cope with unique one-off opportunities such as cross-curricular events, themed weeks and theatre groups?
- Is sufficient attention being placed on children learning to learn and developing the thinking brain?
- Will the curriculum be taught in well managed classrooms that teach pupils about their rights, roles and responsibilities?
- Is sufficient attention being placed on learning styles and the full range of intelligences?

This chapter has argued that the years since 1988 have been a dark period in the context of curriculum design. However in reality there have been rays of light. Head teachers with moral principles and maverick qualities have ensured that they have claimed their autonomy. They have taken full responsibility for curriculum design. When this has been done with conviction and rigour, and when there has been a clear focus on quality, the results have been tremendous. So choose your route, be resolute and select your own destiny. Don't be like Alice.

> Alice reached a crossroads. She asked the Cheshire cat which route she should use. The Cheshire cat said, 'Where do you want to get to?' 'I don't know,' replied Alice. 'Then it doesn't matter which road you take,' said the Cheshire Cat.

Chapter 4

Creating a Vision for Creative Pupils with Creative Teachers in Creative Classrooms

Imagination is more important than knowledge.

Albert Einstein

The Prologue

What's it all about, Alfie?

Springett Lane Junior and Infant School is an **outside in school**. It responds well to the government's initiatives and involves itself in the programmes supplied by the Local Authority. The School Improvement Partners report that the school is working hard and making satisfactory progress. Ofsted say that pupils enter with standards below the national average and they also leave with standards below the national average. In every way Springett Lane Junior and Infant School is average. The head teacher, governors and parents are very pleased that they have embraced all the government and Local Authority initiatives in order to become satisfactory.

It is a summer's evening. Two of the Year 6 pupils have just got off the Yorkshire Traction bus. They are going fishing at a nearby dam. It has been a typical day at school. In a lesson about persuasive writing the children had written a letter complaining about whaling in the Arctic. In history the children had done some work about the ancient Egyptians. Alfie thought this period of history occurred around three hundred years ago and the others had laughed.

It had been a bad day all around for Alfie. He had been sent to the head teacher for swearing in the playground. The dinner lady had brought him in and she was hanging around waiting to see him get a good telling off. When the head teacher asked what he had said Alfie replied that it was too rude to say, so the head had asked for the first letter. Alfie had replied 'N'. The head teacher pointed out he didn't know any swear words beginning with N. Alfie finally admitted to using the word 'knobhead'. The head teacher puzzled over whether he should deal with the spelling issue or the poor language.

This was the first occasion the boys had been fishing for a while because they attended a level 3–4 booster group most evenings. They were now walking through the grounds of a former stately home. Alfie's grandfather had told him that it had the largest house front in Britain and royalty often stayed there prior to going to the St Leger meeting in Doncaster. A famous racehorse called Whistlejacket had been stabled there. It had been painted by a famous artist called Stubbs. King George III was supposed to have been painted with the horse but it reared at the king, who was then left off the painting. Within a one mile radius of where they were standing men, women and children had lost their lives in accidents in coal pits. The 1984 miners' strike had started only three miles to the north. During the strike policemen on horseback charged down miners with batons three miles to the south. Alfie knew bits and pieces of all this. He also knew the names of most of the birds to be found around the dam. He had drawn intricate sketches of many of them.

Alfie imagined what it would be like if these were things he learned about in school. But this will not be, because Springett Lane Junior and Infant is an **outside in school** governed by the frameworks and QCA schemes of work. Don't worry, Alfie, because as Einstein said, 'Imagination is more important than knowledge.'

This chapter focuses on the absolute importance of developing creativity in our primary schools. The text provides a clear model for the development of creativity in your school. It provides monitoring and evaluation tools so that you can explore your current reality in order to establish your vision for the future. The chapter strives to ensure we have creative children taught by creative teachers in creative classrooms.

Philosophy for Children, Thinking Skills, Accelerated Learning, Brain Power, Artsmark and Enterprise Education are phrases which trip of the tongues of many teachers. They have had a significant impact on children as learners over recent years. However there is one word that covers them all: creativity. **Inside out schools** develop creative pupils taught by creative teachers in creative classrooms. Their school leaders see the development of pupil creativity as being an essential part of developing the holistic health and education of the child. This chapter explains why it is important, how to develop it and provides frameworks to help you assess the creativity levels in pupils, teachers and classrooms.

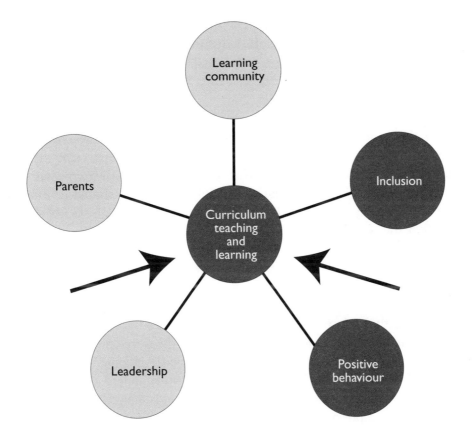

Why creativity is key to learning in inside out schools

Here is a quiz question for the gifted and talented amongst you. Within the last eight years there have been two government backed publications which have stressed the absolute importance of developing pupil creativity. Can you name them? The answer is probably no, because they have been lost in the government's relentless and unimaginative drive to improve test results. This is an absolute tragedy. As a nation we have never truly invested in pupil creativity as an effective form of teaching and learning. As early as 1937 the Board of Education stated:

> The importance of examinations may, on account of the high place it occupies in an unwisely managed school, become unduly exaggerated. ... The fear of an approaching examination has been known to rob school life of a good deal of its spontaneity and freshness.
>
> Board of Education, *Handbook of Suggestions for Teachers* (1937)

This quotation is just as true today. The drive for standards has forced head teachers to play safe. There is insufficient attention placed on creativity and too many lessons are dull and uninspirational. The view that only traditional teaching and three part lessons will lead to good test results is a disease that infects far too many of our schools.

However this is not the case in **inside out schools**. Their head teachers strive to achieve high standards through the development of pupil creativity. We already know that **inside out** head teachers are driven by a moral purpose. They recognise that their pupils have one childhood and it should be magical and wondrous. They are committed to pupil creativity and high standards and believe that the two go hand in hand. Yes, there is a need for direct teaching because discovery favours the well-prepared mind. **Inside out** head teachers believe that there is a clear balance between direct instruction and giving young people the freedom to inquire, question, experiment and express their own thoughts and understanding. Whilst traditional teaching and learning methods have their place in developing basic skills and good learning habits, an over-reliance on such approaches will restrict the development of genuine skills, knowledge, understanding and the holistic development of the child. The worst primary schools are associated with meaningless exercises rather than rich, vivid and real experiences. In these schools Seneca's words become a self-fulfilling prophecy: 'Non vitae sed scholae discimus' (Education is for school and not life).

Too many of our children see school as related to academic life and not real life. So stop and ask yourself two simple questions: When did your teaching last inspire pupils? Do you know what inspirational teaching actually looks like?

I offer a simple response to these questions. Inspirational teaching requires pupils to respond in an inspirational and creative way. Too often this is missing from our schools due to the perceived constraints placed upon them.

Inside out schools place a special emphasis on pupil creativity because they believe it:

- makes primary education enjoyable and memorable
- is the most powerful way of learning
- develops the brain
- motivates young people, raising confidence and self-esteem

- develops skills of communication and social interaction
- encourages tolerance and understanding
- promotes social responsibility
- promotes inclusion rather than exclusion in a world of rapid social and economic change
- increases employability in the longer term

So back to the quiz question. The two government backed publications that have promoted pupil creativity in recent years are *All Our Futures: Creativity, Culture and Education* published by DfES in 1999 and *Creativity: Find It, Promote It* published by QCA in 2001.

Whilst the development of pupil creativity has become constrained in English schools, other countries are moving in the opposite direction. For example, the Norwegian national curriculum suggests that 'education must demonstrate how creative energy and inventiveness have constantly improved the context, content and quality of human life'. Currently Norway gets much of its wealth from North Sea oil but eventually this will run out. The nation knows that creative responses will be required to ensure future wealth.

If an essential part of education is about helping children to achieve well in future life and have good employment opportunities, then schools need to be aware that the creative economy continues to grow faster than other sectors. They also need to be aware of the person specifications in many recruitment advertisements. The desired qualities from a single page of job adverts in a recent newspaper included:

- Capacity to motivate others
- High quality communicator, negotiator and networker
- Ability to thrive in a fast-paced environment
- Confidence within a team
- Flexibility to react to external circumstances
- Confidence, resilience, with superb communication, interpersonal and social skills
- Ability to think creatively and strategically
- PR whiz, media guru, manager, leader and team player all rolled into one (the starting salary for this post was £27,500)

We therefore need a creative and flexible workforce for the future. Schools need to be aware that a significant proportion of pupils entering the foundation stage this year will eventually move into occupations that have not yet been invented. Additionally there could be two or three significant changes in a person's career path during their life in the twenty-first century. The notion that most people will follow a simple career path within a single profession or with a single employer is history.

If we are going to equip children well for this world we need to provide a creative curriculum that:

- leads to more rigorous and critical thinking
- increases motivation and engages more pupils
- improves teacher–pupil and pupil–pupil relationships
- can lead to pupils achieving learning objectives more readily
- requires subject-specific knowledge and skills to flourish and progress

Take some time to reflect on your own educational experiences. Learning should have been a relatively straightforward process. The teacher should have had a clear objective and planned the lesson to ensure that expected gains in learning took place. However, in too many classrooms learning failed to occur because of the contrasting positive and negative forces. Indeed, in too many classrooms where you may have been taught negative forces may have dominated. Think of the occasions when you have been a highly effective learner and then identify three of the common factors. Then consider occasions when you should have been able to learn something but failed. The diagram below reflects the force field of contrasting learning experiences.

A learning force field

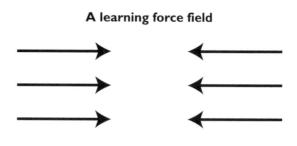

Factors that aid learning   Factors that aid learning

I have used this diagram on many occasions during training sessions. Amongst the common reasons for failing to learn are:

- A learning hierarchy based on age not stage

- An inappropriate emphasis on speed at the expense of quality or thinking time
- An emphasis on preparing for and passing tests
- Fear
- Lack of relevance
- Dull and unimaginative teaching leading to dull and unimaginative recording
- Systems and teachers needs come first and pupil needs come second
- Inappropriate marking and feedback
- A 'dollops curriculum' rather than a coherent curriculum (where you get a dollop of this followed by a dollop of that)

Whereas the reasons for highly effective learning will include:

- Inspirational teaching leading to inspirational learners
- The topic was highly relevant and engaged the emotions
- The lessons stimulated the senses
- Sufficient time was provided for deep learning
- Opportunities were provided for practical activities
- Special relationships within classroom
- Good use of dialogue
- Good use of assessment for learning strategies
- Time for reflection

I believe too many schools have failed to ensure that pupils reach their full potential. In 2003 Catherine Hurley published a book of extracts from school reports of the great and the good. Whilst school reports can say as much about the person writing the report as the subject of the report, the question has to be asked, how many people have been let down by a dull and unimaginative curriculum that was filled with academic exercises rather than being provided with rich and vivid experiences that celebrated the wonder of childhood?

> [John Lennon] Certainly on the road to failure ... hopeless ... rather a clown in class and wastes other pupils' time.

> [Michael Winner] He has the reputation of being movie mad and should try to take up some more creative hobby.

[Judi Dench] Judi would be a very good pupil if only she lived in this world.

[Jilly Cooper] Jilly has set herself an extremely low standard which she has failed to maintain.

Catherine Hurley, Could Do Better:
School Reports of the Great and Good (1997)

A key question that perplexes educationalists is the extent to which heredity and environmental factors influence and shape brain development, learning styles and intelligences. Some people would argue that the research in these areas is full of generalisations. I believe that you dismiss them at your peril, and that the promotion of high quality pupil creativity will develop the academic, practical, emotional and spiritual ability of the child. It also develops the child's brain and therefore helps us to develop children who are better learners.

So use it or lose it. The more we use our brain as we age, the more we encourage it to grow. With high levels of stimulus and challenge there are higher rates of synapses (connections) to the neurons. This means more routes for higher order cognitive functioning. The optimal conditions for such growth would include multiple complex connective challenges where, in learning we are actively engaged in multi sensory immersion experiences.

Alistair Smith, Accelerated Learning in Practice (2000)

Inside out schools develop creative activities will develop both the use of both the left and right hemispheres of the brain

The brain is divided into two hemispheres (left and right) joined by a bridge of fibres. You've all heard how supposedly each hemisphere specialises in different types of thinking and operates in different ways (although this is not entirely neurologically accurate it is useful as a way of thinking about our approach to thinking and learning).

The most effective thinking and learning takes place when there is optimal stimulation to both hemispheres of the brain making them work together in harmony. Accelerated learning will take place through offering creative activities which will stimulate both sides.

However, this can all feel rather clinical. **Inside out schools** believe that the brain will perform best when the heart is fully engaged. In 2006 Dr Andrew Curran stated:

> If you think discipline by force, threat and external rewards, teaching to the brain without going through the heart, and lifeless chalk and talk lessons are the way to teach then think again. After all you don't teach subjects, you teach children.

Andrew Curran, 'How the Brain Works' in
The Big Book of Independent Thinking (2006)

Inside out schools place a strong emphasis on developing whole brain learning by developing pupil creativity. This is because teachers plan materials in ways which stimulate both the left and right brain and engage the senses. This prevents teachers from merely delivering lessons planned to their own hemisphere dominance, which can be the norm. This leads to a balance of right and left brain hemisphere activity in lessons and within the tasks completed by pupils. Effective activities include role play, empathising, discussion and debate, which are proven strategies for securing effective learning. The opportunities must challenge children to take risks with their learning. When children succeed with these challenges it will raise their self-esteem, allowing their neurochemistry to be optimised for future learning.

Inside out schools develop creative activities that will require pupils to use auditory, visual and kinaesthetic learning preferences

The concept of learning preferences is debated by some researchers who argue that there is insufficient evidence about their existence or significance. However, I can make simple observations about both pupils and adults in action to confirm that the vast majority of us have a clear learning preference. Individuals have a tendency to perceive and process information differently as a result of factors such as heredity, upbringing and current environmental demands. The three most commonly identified learning styles are visual, auditory and kinaesthetic. Many researchers believe that each of us will learn best if new knowledge is presented to us in a way that appeals to our learning style preference. This is reflected in the following chart.

Visually oriented learners respond well to	Auditory oriented learners respond well to	Kinaesthetically oriented learners respond well to
The written word	The spoken word	Movement
Diagrams	Lectures	Hands-on activities
Pictures	Audio tapes	Designing and creative activities
Videos	Discussion	Role play and drama
Wall charts and posters	Sound effects	

Be warned: the above information can be misleading if interpreted simplistically. Teachers could take the view that children have a *fixed* learning style and are therefore unable to learn effectively in other ways. In reality, we all need to use a variety of learning styles. Put simply we all need to be able to interpret graphs and charts, listen carefully and carry out practical tasks. In order to do this our learning experiences need to be varied. **Inside out schools** recognise this and seek to develop a clear balance in the learning opportunities offered to children over a week. Currently this is not achieved in many of our schools.

It has been suggested that forty per cent of pupils in our schools are kinaesthetic learners who therefore prefer hands-on practical activities. They are the largest group of children. By contrast thirty-eight per cent of teachers are visual learners and they represent the largest group. There is much evidence to suggest that the majority of lessons have a strong auditory or visual emphasis. This bias has become even more marked since the advent of the literacy and mathematics frameworks. Overall there are inadequate opportunities for kinaesthetic learners to excel and this can lead to a lack of engagement or poor behaviour.

High quality activities aimed at developing learning through pupil creativity will redress this. The best creative activities result in all children using all three of the learning styles, thus helping the child to develop as an all-round learner.

Inside out schools develop creative activities that will develop the full range of intelligences

It has been said that every child born has six significant talents or intelligences. Two come to the surface naturally, two are brought out by other people who are often teachers and the other two remain undiscovered until the person dies. If this is the case, it is extremely sad. The most commonly quoted research within this area was carried out by psychologist Howard Gardner (1984) who identified nine different types of intelligence.

Gardner's intelligences		
Verbal linguistic Facility for word and language in speaking, reading and writing	**Logical mathematical** Capacity for inductive or deductive thinking, use of numbers	**Visual spatial** Ability to visualise objects and spatial dimensions and create internal images
Bodily kinaesthetic High control over physical motion, adept with hands, enjoys active involvement	**Musical rhythmic** Ability to recognise tonal patterns, sensitive to rhythm and beat	**Interpersonal** Strong social skills and relationships, a sensitive listener
Intrapersonal Ability to be reflective and intuitive, self-knowledge and reflection	**Naturalistic** Enjoys outdoors, conducts own enquiries, links learning to natural world	**Existential** Sensitivity, seeks answers to deep questions relating to human existence

Within many of our primary schools there is an excessive focus on verbal linguistic and logical mathematical intelligence. Children who don't perform well within these areas are often labelled as not bright enough. **Inside out schools** believe that:

- **Each child has a unique blend of intelligences**, some of which seem to be natural skills and talents and others that develop largely because of the different life experiences we have.
- **Intelligence is a multiple phenomenon**—individuals make sense of the world and there are many ways in which this can be expressed.
- **Teachers can play a significant part in the development of intelligences** by helping to remove barriers and providing the right range of creative opportunities that develop the full range of intelligences.
- **Assessment procedures should take into account the diversity of intelligences** and thus help children to understand their own special abilities and talents.

Inside out schools will aid pupils to develop all nine intelligences through a creative and informed diversity of teaching and learning opportunities. This is achieved through a carefully thought out, creative, rich, vivid, broad and balanced curriculum that incorporates the arts, self-awareness, communication and physical education. Within this curriculum there will be creative teaching approaches that appeal to all the intelligences, including role play, musical performance, cooperative learning, reflection, visualisation, storytelling and so on.

A definition of creativity

Genuine pupil creativity occurs as a result of a situation where pupils are required to make a unique and original response as a result of careful thought that involves thinking and behaving imaginatively to achieve a clearly defined objective.

However, the definition alone is not powerful enough. I once heard it said that 'creativity without rigour is crap' (I think it was Nietzsche). It has to be absolutely clear that seeking a high quality response from pupils requires high expectations and considerable rigour. In the post-Plowden era of the late 1960s and 1970s there was sometimes a laissez-faire approach to creativity and learning. Often the tasks were undemanding and teachers failed to achieve sufficiently high standards. Creativity is not simply about 'letting the children go'. The best creative experiences require the greatest planning and the highest quality teaching of all. It always arises from a clearly defined learning objective. As a consequence pupils will tackle complex questions and solve challenging problems through ideas that are new to the learner. Children will be challenged throughout the task. At the end of the process the work should be able to stand up to critical evaluation in order to prove that it is of value.

The best pupil creativity is reflected in high quality work that has the following significant features:

- Pride and perseverance
- Originality of thought and effort
- Independence and/or collaboration
- Builds from prior learning
- Helps children to achieve objectives and targets

Introducing the four pillars of creativity in an inside out school

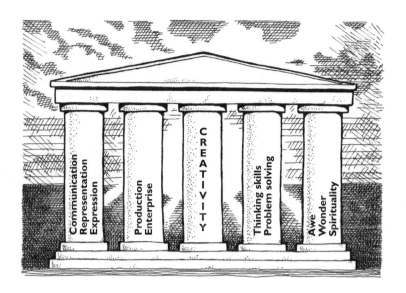

The diagram above represents the four pillars of creativity within an **inside out school**. They are depicted as pillars because if children are allowed to develop the learning skills associated with that particular style of creativity, it will give them strength and support as a learner for the rest of their life—at the same time as providing them with a sense of awe, wonder and spirituality.

Each one will be explained in detail through an investigation of the relationship between creative children taught by the creative teachers in creative classrooms.

First pillar: Communication, representation and expression

> Human life depends upon language, art and the complications of culture as much as on food. It would ultimately collapse without them.
>
> J. Z. Young, *Philosophy and the Brain* (1987)

This pillar is based upon the concept of self-expression. It involves pupils expressing their ideas and feelings in a variety of ways. For more experienced teachers this is the traditional form of creativity they were introduced to at their university or college of education. The expressive arts are the main conduit for this work. This pillar of creativity includes drawing, sketching, painting, sculpture, clay, illustration, dance, photography and written description. The audience for the work is nearly always the teacher who has set a clear task. Learning carried out in this way should always be challenging. However, it is often this strand of work which is seen to have therapeutic qualities, as it allows individuals to respond though their emotions and express their inner feelings.

Whilst this aspect of creativity is considered to be a traditional form of creativity it remains an important part of the work of an **inside out school** in the twenty-first century. This is especially the case in those schools situated within our more deprived communities. In these localities children can have underdeveloped social and emotional skills, and sometimes work within this strand can lead children to develop healthier emotional states because the subconscious becomes expressed rather than suppressed.

As we sail through the sea,
We look in the wobbly water mirror,
People are dreaming about the underwater safari zone,
With coral reefs and jelly fish.
The boats sail yonder on a never-ending diamond.

This piece of writing was produced by an 8-year-old child, who had been on a residential visit. He had then explored the mood of the sea through dance and making music. After these experiences he produced this writing to depict calm seas.

All four pillars of creativity within the **inside out school** are based on a clear and positive relationship between the children, the teacher and the classroom. The following checklist may be helpful in assessing your school's capacity to ensure that creativity is being used successfully to enhance learning within the strand of communication, representation and expression. I suggest you use the following grades: (1) excellent, (2) some good features but further progress is required, and (3) this area is underdeveloped.

First pillar: Communication, representation and expression The children	Grade
The children regularly enjoy listening to stories, music and the views of others	
The children have many opportunities to express their imagination (e.g. storytelling, drama and writing)	
The children regularly communicate in a variety of ways including the spoken word, a range of writing genres, art, dance and music	
The children develop close observational skills that focus on fine detail in art work	
The children develop spoken language and writing skills alongside the observation	
The children use a good range of vocabulary in order to express ideas both verbally and within their writing	
The children regularly draw upon a wide range of experiences in their work	

First pillar: Communication, representation and expression The teacher	Grade
Teachers plan opportunities for thematic work that develops creativity	
Teachers provide an opportunity to develop work from children's needs or interests	
Stories are used as starting points for creative projects	
When working within the creative arts teachers fully explore the links with literacy and numeracy	
Teachers plan circle time and other discussion activities where pupils discuss feelings around difficult issues and each child's contribution is valued and built upon	
The teacher has accessed in-service opportunities in order to promote high quality work within the strand of production, performance and presentation	

First pillar: Communication, representation and expression The classroom	Grade
The classroom has a rich range of resources which aid the development of high quality language work	
Examples of creative writing are shared with pupils and are well displayed within the classroom	
There is a wide range of children's art and 3D work that is well displayed within the classroom	
Where appropriate there are well developed role play areas encouraging imaginative interpretations (including Key Stage 2)	
Resources such as clay are provided to stimulate the imagination	
There is sufficient space, time and commitment for potentially noisy or messy creative activities	
There are also quiet times when children can reflect deeply upon their work and develop strategies for self-improvement	

Creating a Vision for Creative Pupils

Second pillar: Production, performance, presentation and enterprise

If you watch children at play during a weekend or school holiday it is not long before they are organising some kind of production, performance, presentation or event. Some will develop their own dance performances or plays. Alternatively they may develop their own café or shop. Even the football mad boys will organise their own football competitions or devise their own version of the World Cup. Jobs will be allocated and roles will be played. It is a natural part of children growing up. This strand of creativity is based upon this style of learning that comes so readily to children.

The audience for work within this pillar is not simply the teacher. Some form of performance, presentation or event for a wider group of people will be required to conclude the task. However it is not simply about providing the class with a play script and a set of stage directions. Indeed this strand should not just be equated with a drama production. It could be that the task is around planning a display, exhibition, competition or the design of a role play area for others to use within the classroom. Whilst the work could require such essential skills as composing and authorship, it is the actual planning and constant evaluating of the project that is a key element of the learning process. Children will be constantly thinking critically about what is pleasing both to self and others. Within this pillar there are often abundant opportunities to use information and communication technology in exciting, engaging and relevant ways. The four key elements of the creative process will be making, presenting, responding and evaluating. In short assessment for learning strategies will be high profile. The opportunities within this strand will lead to a dynamic interaction between the work and those who engage in it.

The children will have considerable bursts of energy within this kind of work. However, there will be periods when the ideas run short and the teacher will need to be there to provoke further thought through carefully considered questions. It is not simply a case of launching a project and letting the children go. These kinds of creative activities require high quality planning. It will also be a useful strategy if teachers record the learning as it goes along. Moments of clear learning and originality can easily be lost. The ready availability of digital photography can be very useful in this context.

The following checklist may be helpful in assessing your school's capacity to ensure that creativity is being used successfully to enhance learning within the strand of production, performance and presentation. As previously, I suggest you use the following grades: (1) excellent, (2) some good features but further progress is required, and (3) this area is underdeveloped.

Second pillar: Production, performance and presentation The children	Grade
The children get regular opportunities to plan and present their own work to a wider audience	
There are sufficient opportunities for children to fully develop their own ideas in an individual, original and imaginative way when producing and presenting their work	
Children show high levels of independence, pride and perseverance within the process of a task	
Children contribute effectively to discussions within the process of a task	
There are opportunities for children to feel a strong sense of ownership in their work	

Second pillar: Production, performance and presentation The teacher	Grade
Teachers use a variety of teaching styles and techniques to develop pupils' creativity	
Teachers have high expectations that allow pupils to take full responsibility for planning and presenting their work in a range of creative ways	
Teachers regularly encourage children to share their ideas in learning	
Genuine time is allowed for children to develop and modify their ideas	
The teacher has accessed in-service opportunities in order to promote high quality work within the strand of production, performance and presentation	

Second pillar: Production, performance and presentation The classroom	Grade
The classroom is a creative place where pupils regularly present and exhibit their work in a creative way	
The classroom is designed for, and encourages, meaningful pupil collaboration	
Displays in the classroom reflect both individual and group work	
Examples of process are displayed (such as photographs, sketches or draft copies) which show the learning processes used by the children	
These classroom displays are sometimes planned by the children and reflect the learning processes they have gone through	
Displays and exhibitions of pupils' creativity are labelled so that children, parents and governors are aware of the processes within the strand	

Creating a Vision for Creative Pupils

CASE STUDY

One particularly interesting enterprise activity I have seen in primary schools is the five pound challenge. In this activity each child in the class is given a £5 note, but they are told that they have to find a way of making it grow so that in a month's time they hand back more than £5. Before long children are exploring business opportunities and many realise the value of collaborating and starting their own company. Whatever activity the children carry out must be done in a business-like way and nothing should be provided free of charge.

One class were told that at the end of term they had to run a restaurant for a day and that it had to make a profit. The children spent the term following programmes of study that would equip them for the task. They visited restaurants, set up a business contract with the school kitchen, booked a four-piece orchestra for background music, divided up roles and responsibilities and developed strategies for advertising.

Third pillar: Originality, thinking skills and problem solving

> Classrooms should be places where thinking, questioning, predicting, contradicting and doubting is not only tolerated but actively pursued.
>
> Carol McGuiness, *From Thinking Skills to Thinking Classrooms:*
> *A Review for Developing Approaches for Developing Thinking* (1999)

This strand of creativity is based on developing originality of thought, problem solving and cognition through activities which genuinely make the brain work. Focusing on thinking skills in classrooms supports active cognitive processing which makes for better learning. It aids children in developing a critical attitude to information and argument as well as aiding them to communicate effectively. **Inside out schools** see learners as active creators of their own knowledge. Thinking will be promoted through *sequencing and sorting, classifying and comparing, making predictions, relating cause and effect, drawing conclusions, generating new ideas, problem solving, testing solutions and making decisions*. The best thinking activities are based around learning tasks that are not routine but have a high degree of open-endedness and uncertainty and therefore produce multiple solutions. Learners should be allowed time to talk about their learning processes in order to make them more explicit. During problem solving activities dialogue with the teacher or adults is equally important as it allows for pupil reflection.

This form of creativity is high profile in the national curriculums of many other countries. For example, in Singapore thirty per cent of time is given to this type of work. This is because they believe their future as an economy and a nation rests not on getting people to a high level in narrow fields but on developing creative individuals who are empowered in their creative thinking and their ability to create their own future. Creative thought shapes our future.

> The greatest advancements over the last 100 years such as the light bulb, the computer and the airplane were created by innovators, people who imagined things that did not exist—and asked why...
>
> Bernie Milano

Persevering with thought is also essential. The Wright brothers are normally credited with the invention of the airplane, although others were better placed to succeed with man-powered flight. The Wright brothers had many crashes and each crash brought profound learning. In short they persevered with their thinking.

Wilbur Wright, considered to be the brother with vision, worked alongside Orville Wright, the brother who loved to tinker. Wilbur once said, 'My brother Orville and myself lived together, played together and, in fact, thought together.' Wilbur and Orville persevered in their struggle against Mother Nature, public opinion and failed flights to fulfil their dream of making a flying machine. Their airplane started out as a glider, then it evolved into a plane that stayed in the air for five seconds and finally into a plane that stayed in the air for one hour and thirteen minutes.

The Wright brothers were school dropouts. Perhaps they never received the stimulating challenges they needed or had the capacity to resolve. Schools need to be places where originality of thought is fully embraced. The more we use our brains the more we encourage them to grow. Higher rates of stimulus and challenge lead to higher rates of cognitive functioning.

The following checklist may be helpful in assessing your school's capacity to ensure that creativity is being used successfully to enhance learning within the strand of originality and problem solving. As previously, I suggest you use the following grades: (1) excellent, (2) some good features but further progress is required, and (3) this area is underdeveloped.

Third pillar: Thinking skills and problem solving The children	Grade
Children regularly respond to problem solving challenges with enthusiasm	
Children welcome new ideas and situations	
The children persevere in order to find solutions	
Skills and techniques are used in unusual ways	
Children enjoy working with others to solve problems and also work through their ideas alone	
Children evaluate and refine the ideas of others	
Children regularly carry out mathematical investigations in a creative way	
Children carry out their own scientific investigations	
The children use ICT to help them to solve problems or refine their thinking	
The children carry out high quality design technology work	
The children express their ideas orally	

Third pillar: Thinking skills and problem solving The teacher	Grade
The work is planned to encourage adaptability and so that children can transfer learning from one subject area to another	
The teacher provides a balance between closed and open-ended activities	
The teacher provides encouragement for pupils who show exceptional ability	
The teacher ensures that children are encouraged to take risks and that they feel supported on these occasions	
The teacher has accessed in-service opportunities in order to promote high quality work within thinking skills and problem solving	

Third pillar: Thinking skills and problem solving The classroom	Grade
The learning environment provides a secure basis for risk taking	
Children can readily access appropriate mathematical resources	
The classroom has a suitable range of science resources	
The classroom allows for large scale construction play, designing and making	
The classroom has interactive and thought provoking displays	
The interactive whiteboard is used to develop thinking skills and problem solving in a creative way	

Fourth pillar: Universe, creation, awe and wonder

For many with whom I have worked, this fourth strand of creativity is more abstract; however, to me it is absolutely essential. Creativity and creation come together as a source of wonder and inspiration. This strand of creativity is about children and teachers working in a more holistic way using the world around them to inspire creative learning. The underlying principle is that the classroom should have no walls and that learning should regularly take place outside. This provides a different emotional and spiritual climate which allows creative thought to flourish as a result of access to the rich world in which we live. This form of creative thought can never develop from a textbook or the internet. Working through first hand experiences ensures that children use rich sensory images of the world and thus focus intently. It helps to create a clear sense of awe and wonder and develop spiritual intelligence. First hand experiences can stay with the child for life, not just in terms of shapes, colours or textures; there can be a totality of recall that will never be the same if derived from a second hand experience.

Teachers need to be able to see the potential of using the outside as a creative learning resource. Traditionally we expected children to learn indoors and to play outdoors (often in sterile environments). Teachers have always been aware of the influence of outside factors such as the weather on children. They are always more difficult to handle on wet days and excitable on snowy days. Therefore they should take full advantage of misty days, frosty days, autumnal days, windy days and stormy days as motivation for the children within writing, speaking and listening, art, music and drama. In such conditions the children are more emotionally charged, making them more enthusiastic and motivated.

One school I have recently visited has developed a school allotment where the children grow a variety of fruits and vegetables from seed. For many inner city children this remains a magical experience. They are fully responsible for their care and for harvesting when the growing period is over. The crops are then presented to the school cook who works with the children to prepare dishes for school dinners. This is an absolutely wonderful holistic experience for children, which through creative activity provokes awe and wonder and helps children to make sense of creation within the world around them. We must ask the question: If we, as teachers, don't create such a sense of awe, wonder and spirituality in our pupils, then who will?

> Creativity is not always dependent upon sophisticated resources; indeed quite the opposite can be true. The wind can provide a simple and free resource to explore sound, movement and natural forces. The plants grown in a school garden cost no more than the packets of seeds. Yet they provide simple and stimulating opportunities for understanding the growth of living things. Earth, water, air, the weather, light and sound are all around us and freely available. Responding to these elements provides the children with almost the only resources they will need to begin to create for themselves from their own images.
>
> F. Beetlestone, *Creative Children, Imaginative Teaching* (1998 [1980])

However, not all of this can be achieved merely within the school grounds. Children not only need to be taken to places of outstanding beauty, but also to experience the wonders of man-made environments. They should also consider the less desirable issues within our world such as pollution and global warming. I recently visited a school in South Yorkshire where a class had gone on a cliff top walk in Whitby, seen the mighty River Don steam engine in action at a Sheffield museum and looked at derelict buildings following the closure of a local factory. All of these stimuli required the children to respond in creative ways, leading them to make sense of the world around them, and thus develop spiritual intelligence.

I hope the links between creativity and the natural and man-made world as a source of inspiration are clearer. The creative use of the external world for a child can be a source of great motivation. The four walls of the classroom can also be a considerable constraint. Where children and teachers respond creatively with their surroundings they are both contented and motivated. Children's physical, emotional and spiritual development can be nurtured alongside their creative development by making full use of the environment. Many of the resources are free and simply waiting to be used to enhance learning across the curriculum and improve the quality of life for learners—and teachers—within this mad age of **outside in schools**.

The following checklist may be helpful in assessing your school's capacity to ensure that creativity is being used successfully to enhance learning within the strand of universe, creation, awe and wonder. As previously, I suggest you use the following grades: (1) excellent, (2) some good features but further progress is required, and (3) this area is underdeveloped.

Fourth pillar: Universe, creation, awe and wonder The children	Grade
Children draw upon aspects of the natural world to aid creative expression	
Children draw upon aspects of the man-made world to aid creative expression	
Children demonstrate aspects of creativity in different environmental settings including the classroom, playground and local visits	
Children develop close observational skills including presenting in detail small parts of a larger object	
Children develop descriptive language alongside these observations	
Children demonstrate wonder, amazement and enthusiasm for learning	

Fourth pillar: Universe, creation, awe and wonder The teacher	Grade
Teachers have freedom in the curriculum to respond to changes in seasons or the weather	
Teachers regularly create opportunities for children to respond to the natural environment and to focus on plants and animals using multi sensory skills	
Teachers regularly create opportunities for children to respond to the man-made environment	
Teachers plan cause and effect activities	
Teachers develop children's sensitivity to weather, mood and atmospheres, increasing their ability to respond emotionally and spiritually	

Fourth pillar: Universe, creation, awe and wonder The classroom	Grade
Teaching and learning frequently takes place in outside areas and away from the school site	
The classroom reflects an appreciation of the natural and human world through its provision of resources, artefacts and visual imagery	
Children are encouraged to use their creativity to develop their own local environments (classrooms, school grounds or community spaces)	

Creating the vision for creativity

Head teachers often speak with passion about the absolute significance of pupil creativity. However, this passion is not always tuned in to the appropriate actions. If you want pupil creativity to be an essential part of your school curriculum, the following questions may be helpful in moving your school forward:

- Does the school improvement plan place an appropriate emphasis on developing learning from creative partnerships?
- Is the importance of creativity reflected in the appropriate sections of the Ofsted Self-Evaluation Form?
- Does the school have appropriate measures for assessing pupil creativity?
- How does the school organisation and management promote creativity?
- Does the school plan professional learning opportunities to enhance creativity?
- Do the school's accommodation and resources effectively promote creativity?
- Does the school access links with other organisations in order to develop high quality creativity?
- Has your school identified key priorities for the year ahead in order to further develop pupil creativity?

Having completed the checklist for developing creative pupils taught by creative teachers in creative classrooms now consider in broad terms what your school will be like in three years' time.

 Now state how your school will be different in one year's time.

_____

_____

As you move towards achieving your vision you may find the chart below helpful in identifying areas where high quality practice is developing and also where further work is required.

	Rarely promotes imaginative activity leading to outcomes that are of originality and value	Sometimes promotes imaginative activity leading to outcomes that are of originality and value	Regularly promotes imaginative activity leading to outcomes that are of originality and value
Foundation Stage			
Key Stage 1			
Lower Key Stage2			
Upper Key Stage 2			
English			
Mathematics			
Science			
ICT			
Religious Education			
Geography			
History			
Art			
Music			
Design Technology			
Physical Education			
Primary Languages			
Other aspect 1			
Other aspect 2			
Other aspect 3			

Creating a Vision for Creative Pupils

Inside out schools place a high priority on creativity within a personalised curriculum. They see it as the cornerstone of an inspirational curriculum led by inspirational teachers who provide activities that lead to inspirational pupils who will achieve high standards. These schools know that it is absolutely essential to reach the right balance between providing appropriate instruction and providing the children with the opportunity to construct their own learning. **Inside out schools** see the curriculum not as a body of knowledge but as a source of enquiry. They believe in valuing childhood as a period of wonder and imagination. They regularly reflect on the words of Einstein at the opening of this chapter:

Imagination is more important than knowledge.

Chapter 5

Creating a Vision for the Best Classrooms

Without an understanding of what the brain was designed to do in the environment in which we evolved, the unnatural activity called education is unlikely to succeed.

Stephen Pinker

The Prologue

Clipboards, Pandas and Supermarkets

It was 8.30 a.m. and I was standing in the reception area of a primary school waiting to see the head teacher prior to carrying out a monitoring visit for a newly qualified teacher. Whilst this is often a great privilege, my presence often places an immense strain upon the teacher. Many people say that the driving test is the most stressful examination of all. It is based on a one-to-one situation where you deal with unknown traffic conditions and all your judgements and actions have to be totally coordinated whilst sitting in the company of an unknown stranger. For some people even greater stress occurs when you have to teach a class of thirty, sometimes unpredictable, children in front of an Ofsted inspector or a Local Authority adviser.

The visit took place during the early days of the National Literacy Strategy when many lessons followed a particular model of word or sentence level work followed by a main theme and a plenary. To be quite honest, I had already grown tired of the model and was fearful that I was about to see a rather dull lesson. Some of the textbook publishers had already weighed in providing banks of unimaginative exercises which years and years of educational research had shown to be of little value. However, as I entered the classroom I immediately perked up. This was clearly a lively and vibrant classroom and the children were soon bounding through the door. They were clearly supportive of each other and wanted to do well for their teacher who had already told them that they had a special visitor.

However, the lesson that followed, which was about persuasive writing, didn't seem to follow the norm for this classroom. This apparently vibrant young teacher took the children through a relatively mundane lesson relating to saving pandas followed by traditional exercises from published photocopiable worksheets. Teacher talk dominated and there was very little opportunity for dialogue. There was a poor response rate to the many closed questions as children saw little relevance in the exercise and had little emotional involvement in the lesson. It was clear that the children were relatively confused by what was going on. They were clearly used to a much richer diet. The evidence around me in the classroom suggested that their teacher usually believed that if you couldn't see it, touch it or smell it, then it was too abstract and didn't belong in the primary classroom.

After the lesson finally came to a close it was time to offer feedback. I referred to the then useful Ofsted framework for grading lessons which stressed 'the importance of using imaginative resources that makes intellectual and creative demands on pupils to extend their learning and as a consequence, pupils are keen to learn, rise to challenges in creative ways and think further.' At this point the teacher stopped the proceedings and asked if she could describe the lesson that she had originally planned to do. This involved a large multinational supermarket chain which was seeking to purchase the school playing field to develop a new store. She had planned for a local pensioner to come into the classroom to defend the store saying she would welcome local access to fresh produce. A councillor from the governing body was going to express his concerns for the plans. Drama and hot seating was planned and before long this young teacher was making the hairs on the back of my head stand on end. I started excitedly chipping in with my own suggestions. The original plan sounded fabulous.

I asked the inevitable question: why hadn't she carried out the lesson? She looked at me sadly with hesitation in her eyes and said, 'Because you were coming and I was frightened it may not work or that you wouldn't like it because it wasn't a three-part lesson.' I suddenly realised that my presence with a clipboard had the potential to drain the confidence out of a teacher. This was brought home to me on another occasion when I led a staff meeting aimed at raising the quality of teaching and learning prior to an Ofsted inspection. The staff watched a video of a young teacher who had taken a group of children onto the school field to study seed dispersal. One teacher, in the image of Les Dawson—with a face like a bag of spanners and her handbag on her knee—adjusted her bust and said, 'As if you would do that during an Ofsted inspection.' Children need exciting, lively, relevant and engaging lessons at all times. Classrooms and lessons must promote practical, emotional and spiritual intelligence as well as academic learning. The system we work within must promote confidence rather than drain it out of teachers.

This chapter will help you to create a vision for providing high quality learning environments. Over recent years there has been an investment in classrooms and the science of pedagogy. There has been a significant drive on setting targets for pupils' learning so that they know the next steps. The use of objectives has added precision to teaching. There has been considerable guidance on dialogue and questioning. The role of the plenary has been stressed. Lessons are now aided by interactive whiteboards and other new technologies. Teachers have never been better technically or technologically equipped. This chapter takes the thinking even further. It stresses the need to ensure that whatever happens within your school's classroom matches what we know about the human brain and the way in which children learn.

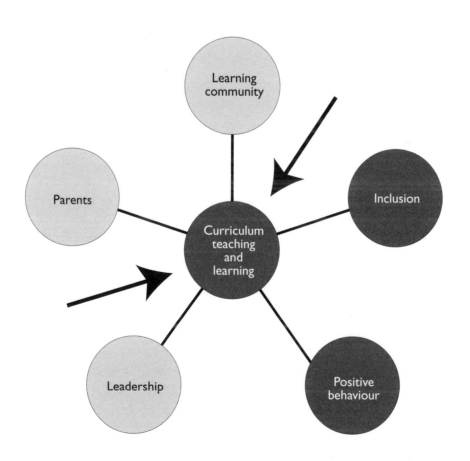

Why the classroom is so important

The best **inside out teachers** love their classroom. As they close the door, tired and exhausted on a Friday evening, they turn back and look at it one more time. Their eyes are drawn towards a significant display or piece of work from the week. It provides a sense of pride and enjoyment. It is a reflection of both the school's and the individual teacher's educational philosophy. It provides a clear insight into the teacher's love and commitment to primary education.

There is an argument that says that the classroom is noted for constancy in the face of change. The basic classroom is remarkably similar across the world and has changed little over time. Research into teaching and learning has often had very little impact on classroom design and practice. However the **inside out school leader** recognises that the classroom is a highly important factor in school improvement. This has been confirmed by research into school effectiveness which has recognised that it is classrooms that have the major impact on the performance of pupils. It is classrooms that explain much more of the variation in pupil performance than overall school policy. For example:

> Recent research on the impact of schools on student learning leads to the conclusion that 8–19% of the variation in student learning outcomes lies between schools and a further amount of up to 55% of the variation in individual learning outcomes between classrooms within schools.
>
> Paul Cuttance, 'Quality Assurance Reviews as a Catalyst for School Improvement in Australia', in A. Hargreaves, A. Lieberman, M. Fullan and D. Hopkins (eds), *The International Handbook of Educational Change* (1998)

> Studies of school effectiveness and school improvement indicate that the classroom effect is greater than the whole school effect in explaining student progress.
>
> Louise Stoll, 'Realising Our Potential: Understanding and Developing Capacity for Lasting Improvement', *School Effectiveness and School Improvement* (1999)

There have been many studies into the different influences on student learning. One study examined 11,000 variables and concluded that two consistent and significant themes arise in developing high quality learning—these are classroom management and metacognitive processes.

Another study showed that pupils' views about their personal attributes and about others, about how the world works and what is important in life, combined with metacognition, were the key drivers in developing effective learning in classrooms. It is therefore essential to focus on classrooms because that is where these views are formed and learning actually takes place. It is here that teachers have an impact on learners' beliefs and thinking. Furthermore, if the key factors that bring success are pupil self-esteem and metacognition, it is essential to focus on our knowledge of how the human brain works and functions, and create classrooms that aid this.

Fitting the classroom to the brain

The challenge therefore becomes to create a classroom around the way in which the brain functions. Every aspect of a child's behaviour in the classroom relates to the way in which the teacher either feeds or starves the brain. If the child smiles, laughs, cares for others and loves learning, it is due to the way in which the teacher successfully makes the brain function and develop. However, it is also the case that where children misbehave, forget things or fail as learners it is potentially due to the way in which teachers have closed down the brain. I once heard a highly influential school inspector say that teachers should be made to consume their own smoke in terms of poor behaviour. After approximately 140 years of compulsory education, primary school teachers still know very little about how the brain works. This is because it has never been a significant part of initial teacher training and it has been approached in many schools as an ad hoc form of continuing professional development.

However, the best teachers have always had a strong element of instinct and have provided the right types of environments where minds have been opened and optimal learning has taken place. As a consequence children have flourished. These teachers often have a wonderful unwarranted optimism in what children can achieve and the pupils have risen to the challenge. These teachers create the *hopeful classroom culture*.

Other teachers have brought fear and conflict into classrooms. Their expectations are not high enough to allow pupils to take responsibility. Teacher talk dominates along with closed tasks done largely for the teacher. I regard this as the *woeful classroom culture* and for many pupils it is particularly damaging. When a doctor joins the medical profession they are required to take the Hippocratic Oath, which means that first and foremost they must do no harm. There are still far too many teachers who harm the minds of our youngsters on a daily basis. As I get older my tolerance of these people grows weaker. The **inside out school leader** will work hard with these teachers, but if necessary seek to rid the profession of such people.

Key features of the hopeful classroom culture
• There are very many different ways to learn
• Effective learners take responsibility for their own learning
• Learning takes place within a social context
• Speech and dialogue are key processes within learning
• Mistakes are an integral part of the learning process
• Effort should be rewarded within learning
• There is no tension between pupils and teachers
• Positive exchanges predominate

Key features of the woeful classroom culture
• Learning is done best on your own and carried out in silence
• It is getting it right (preferably first time) that counts
• It is the teacher's job to impart learning
• All learners can be classed as able, average or less able
• Teachers believe that some children aren't good at learning
• There are moments of stress, tension and shouting between teachers and pupils and vice versa
• Teacher talk dominates as a form of presenting information

Classroom practice and the reptilian brain

The first challenge is to ensure that the reptilian brain is catered for. This part of the brain is responsible for the regular body functions which operate without our conscious awareness (such as breathing, blood pressure and balance). It also takes charge at times of anxiety and stress. In order for effective learning to take place physical and emotional needs must be satisfied. Stressful conditions activate the reptilian brain and close down the brain's higher order functions. In a classroom context this would include times when there is a lack of self-esteem, a feeling of insecurity or isolation, fear of failure or disparagement, personal worries or a sense of injustice. The following checklists indicate the key features that all classrooms need to adopt to keep the reptilian brain happy. You can establish your current reality and establish what needs to change in the future.

Do your classrooms pass the reptilian brain checklist?	Present/ Not present
Each pupil has their own territory such as a drawer, locker and coat peg.	
All aspects of physical comfort (such as appropriate warmth, light, etc.) and an absence of thirst or hunger are met.	
All the children feel valued and welcomed. Teachers trained to Montessori principles recognise the absolute value of welcoming every child into the classroom. For many, spoken words are not even necessary—simply standing by the door offering a smile and eye contact works wonders.	
There are clear routines particularly at times of transition where pupils move around the building and at the start and end of lessons so that children clearly anticipate what happens next.	
Teachers are absolutely certain about what they expect from children through setting the right achievable goals and targets.	
Opportunities exist to bring a sense of identity and belonging, such as assemblies, having a class name, mission and rules or school teams and houses.	
Children feel physically and emotionally safe as a result of the effective use of praise. In our most positive learning environments the positive exchanges outnumber the negative by at least five to one.	
Opportunities exist to develop both the social and emotional intelligence of pupils. Pupils are allowed opportunities to talk about their feelings and be taught how to manage them. Children should also be taught how to build relationships and deal with conflict. Classrooms are free of sarcasm and insults and are places that are fair and consistent.	

 Now state what will be different in three years' time.

 Now state what will be different in one year's time.

The government has recognised the importance of the social and emotional aspects of learning through the Social and Emotional Aspects of Learning (SEAL) programme which has been implemented in many primary schools. This work has a tremendous capacity to reach right across the curriculum. SEAL promotes certain key features which aim at keeping the reptilian brain happy. For example, many classrooms now have mood boards where children declare how they are feeling as they enter the classroom. If they declare that they are worried, angry or sad it allows time for a teacher, learning mentor or teaching assistant to discuss the pupil's concerns, hopefully disarming the reptilian brain and enabling purposeful work to follow.

Classroom practice and the limbic system

The limbic system is in the mid brain and governs learning, memory and emotions. **Inside out school leaders** recognise the absolute importance of this part of the brain. It is responsible for character building. It creates a sense of values and establishes our beliefs. It attaches truth to what we learn and helps us to develop a sense of self. Our longer term memory is situated within the limbic system. Research shows that emotions are fundamentally important in learning, and the more powerfully emotions are connected to the information we need to learn, the quicker it will become embedded in our memory, and the easier it becomes to recall. High levels of teacher talk and traditional exercises will not enable the limbic system to develop deep learning. However, the following classroom practices trigger highly effective learning.

- When introducing new learning teachers will involve pupils in prediction exercises and the making and sharing of mind maps.
- Skilful teachers scaffold learning through high quality dialogue, role play, discussion groups or the exciting use of an interactive whiteboard. Working and speaking with other pupils develops a shared consciousness though group interaction and a borrowed consciousness from other more expert pupils.
- Classrooms with 'no walls', where external environments are used to create a sense of awe and wonder, and learning is seen as searching to create meaning from our environment. **Inside out schools** recognise that the daily need for outside education at the Foundation Stage does not suddenly disappear on the first Monday in September when the child enters Key Stage 1. Design problems can provide problems for many schools, but

simple patio doors opening onto decking or garden/allotment areas could be a fabulous starting point.

- Stimuli such as humour, music, colour or an element of surprise are used to engage learners.
- Teachers develop ways of summarising work that involve visualisation and pupil dialogue in which children review their own learning.

Classroom practice and brain lateralisation

Although it is not strictly neurologically accurate it can be a useful metaphor to consider that the brain is divided into two hemispheres joined by a bridge of fibres which allow both sides of the brain to work together. Each hemisphere serves a variety of different functions and processes information in different ways. For most people, the left hemisphere deals with linguistic issues. It is analytical and is therefore used extensively in problem solving activities or when sequential processing is required. If the left brain is analytical, logical, precise and time-sensitive then the right brain sees the bigger picture, processing things in a holistic way. It is also more emotional. It thrives on rhythm and music and learns well from images and pictures.

Using the left brain/right brain theory as an analogy, it can be said that individuals tend to 'favour' one way of processing information and can be thought of as left brain or right brain people. This has implications for the classroom where pupils who prefer processing information with their left brain often do better than those who prefer the right hemisphere (sometimes these could be children struggling with their learning, boys, or even potentially more able pupils). It also has implications for the way in which you teach. Teachers often interpret data, represent data and provide learning experiences based on that data in their own preferred way.

The right-brained person often works from intuition. As a right brained person I can visit IKEA and bring home the self-assembly bookshelves and put them up in a highly effective manner without resorting to any instruction book. I know I can do this well because I can complete the task and still have nine bits left over. It has been claimed that left-brained people often prefer a learning environment that is quiet, brightly lit and has a formal layout. They often prefer to learn from an authority figure. By contrast, right-brained people prefer dimmer lighting, an informal design and peer interaction.

However, this would not reflect a typical primary classroom and there is clear evidence that too many classrooms favour left-brained pupils. This is both in their layout and through their focus on reading, writing and mathematics, which are often presented in a verbal manner. In reality it has always been this way. Too many schools and teachers take the traditional view of students as being a homogenous learning group, with similar interests in—and aptitudes for—the subject. However, greater learning and understanding may be accomplished if the learning group is thought of as being heterogeneous, that is highly dissimilar in interest and aptitudes. The chart below can be useful for teachers and school leaders to assess the balance between right-brained and left-brained activities within their classroom. Teachers should simply consider the lessons and activities they have planned and taught over the last two weeks and match them to the appropriate box below. When this is complete they should consider the balance between the activities and any implications relating to their classroom practice. School leaders can also carry out the exercise to gain a whole school view.

Activities which were predominantly teacher led learning within traditional classroom structure and organisation	
Activities based on discovery, methods based on collaboration and dialogue and flexible classroom organisation	
Implications	

If we accept the theory of left–right brain hemisphere dominance and learning styles then there are profound implications for education. As stated previously, our classrooms are largely geared to left-brained people, yet it is the right-brained people who are more likely to be creative and innovative. Equally right-brained people need left-brained activity if they are to bring order and structure to their sometimes chaotic minds. The best classrooms provide opportunities for both sides of the brain to work together.

> The curriculum does not help students to become more intelligent because it is too knowledge based. You need to trigger the right brain to create the smart successful learner.
>
> Middlewood, Parker and Beere, *Creating a Learning School* (2005)

The problem is that all of this can become rather dangerous and before long people are almost excused from tasks because they prefer using either their left or right brain hemisphere. It should be absolutely clear that both hemispheres are important and need to be used. It is not better to be a right-brained or a left-brained learner. However, it is very possible that there is a regular mismatch between many learners' preferences and the learning experience being offered. The best informed teachers and school leaders have an understanding of the brain and its design and seek to develop whole brain learning activities. The first challenge is to ensure that pupils receive a balanced diet. Too much emphasis on either hemisphere leads to an impoverished learning diet. Secondly, and more importantly, teachers need to make the two sides of the brain work together. This means offering activities which stimulate both sides. Simple use of music and visual imagery is one way but the real answer lies in providing rich and vivid creative activities for pupils. These were explored in greater detail in Chapter 4. However, when teachers employ the following principles they will be starting to create classrooms that are focused on whole brain learning:

1. Learning is best when there is an emotional involvement that involves the heart as well as the head. Firstly this can come from the content of the lesson. As a teacher working predominantly in areas around the former South Yorkshire coal field I am amazed by the attention given to more abstract periods of history while paying no attention to the miners' strike which is an issue which really would engage the emotions and provide a genuine sense of identity.

2. Teachers need to constantly promote and teach children to be motivated and have high self-esteem as this will have a positive effect on their behaviour and capacity to learn. This includes the promotion of positive and supportive relationships and ethos.

3. Learning should always be an interactive process. To build cognitive structures and concepts we need to use new experiences from earlier learning. Effective teaching recognises the critical role played by experiences and interactions with the surrounding environment.

4. Learning should always be seen as a social process because working with others through genuine dialogue provides greater knowledge and understanding. This is as a result of shared consciousness from the group interaction and also borrowed consciousness as a result of working with others with greater expertise. When used effectively children will learn far more from this approach than learning alone. Effective teachers use group and paired work to scaffold and support learning. **Inside out schools** recognise that the derivation of the word 'dialogue' relates to conversation aimed at achieving understanding

5. Effective teaching promotes explicit reflection on learning through meta-cognitive processes. Children should be encouraged to reflect on what they already know, and what they need to learn next. They should also develop their own strategies for accessing this learning. Children need to have a variety of problem solving techniques that they can apply in a range of contexts.

6. The best learning requires the brain to process information. Direct instruction has a clear role. Teachers and learners cannot cope with open-ended discovery methods all the time. There is nothing wrong with some direct whole class teaching. However, it is essential to use the right questions and follow-up activities that allow the mind to process information.

7. Learning should always be seeking to promote independent pupils who achieve well as a result of carefully structured learning experiences.

8. Whilst clear learning objectives are usually declared through WALT (We are learning to) and the intended outcomes through WILF (What I am looking for), which both favour the logical left brain, the WiiFM (What's in it for me?) is often ignored. This helps to paint the big picture within the right hemisphere of the brain by pointing out the advantages of learning this new technique or skill.

9. ICT resources should be used in an effective manner. They can be used in a systematic way that supports processing information in a logical way. They can be used to provide visualisation and also to provide creative and problem solving opportunities which favour the right brain.

10. Children create meaning from an interaction with their environment. This means there is a need not only for all classrooms to be high quality

learning environments, but also a need to ensure that children learn from experiences outdoors.

Learning environments

As a result of the factors discussed, **inside out school leaders** believe that there are several fundamental factors that contribute to effective classrooms and contribute to whole brain learning. These include:

- A clear set of values, principles and beliefs that exist in all aspects of classroom life that are articulated and modelled on all occasions.
- The promotion of the emotional well-being of the full classroom community.
- Highly effective relationships between adults with adults, adults with children and children with children.
- A shared understanding of the rights and responsibilities of all members of the classroom community.
- Effective relationships with the wider community (parents, carers and other professional agencies).
- A clear system for promoting good behaviour, attendance and punctuality.
- Ensuring there is no bullying or discrimination.
- Promoting a respect for the learning environment so that it remains organised and cared for.

Inside out schools promote the importance of effective learning environments that are clean, tidy and stimulate high quality learning. The following checklist may be helpful in analysing your classroom or school. Whilst it could be used as a monitoring tool it has also been used powerfully as a resource for peer mentoring or coaching activities between members of staff. When used in this way, colleagues could spend time in each other's classrooms observing lessons or even team teaching, and use the checklist to promote further developments in the learning environment. Alternatively the checklist could be used during a learning walk around the school. The leadership team or continuing professional development coordinator could spend ten to fifteen minutes in each classroom and complete the checklist prior to moving on to the next part of the school. It is important to do this straight away so that key elements do not become forgotten.

A checklist for classroom environments that promote whole brain learning	Comments
Learning objectives are displayed and used and children are fully aware of what is in it for them	
Key questions, prompts and scaffolds are available to support children's dialogue and thinking about learning	
Curriculum displays include statements and questions to highlight the key learning points	
The layout of the classroom allows for interactive teaching	
Seating and tables are used flexibly to support working in different contexts and for different purposes	
The layout of the classroom and provision and access to resources supports both independent and collaborative learning	
Displays reflect the learning process across the curriculum	
High quality finished work that reflects pride and perseverance, originality and creativity, independence and collaboration, and building on prior learning are displayed in a sensitive manner	
Displays also reflect and support on-going learning through techniques such as working walls	
Metacognitive displays remind children of strategies that make them effective learners	
There are positive affirmations that raise self-esteem. These could celebrate children achieving their targets, moving towards their targets or the opportunity for pupils to nominate their 'star of the day'	

A checklist for classroom environments that promote whole brain learning (*continued*)	Comments
Diversity is celebrated in all forms. For example, resources including books and visual images reflect the family lives of pupils and their communities	
Resources are well organised, labelled and accessible to pupils who can select when to use them	
There are a range of books that are attractively displayed, well organised and readily accessible to the children	
Children regularly get opportunities to work outdoors and in the wider environment as well as in the classroom	
ICT resources are available in the classroom and are used regularly by adults and teachers to promote ICT as a way of learning across the curriculum	
Space is well used to promote seamless working and the classroom is clean and tidy to promote a sense of pride	

 Now state in broad terms how the school's learning environments will be different in three years' time.

What will be different in one year's time?

Summary

The term 'personalisation' has gone through many interpretations in primary education. Twenty years ago children often ploughed through commercially produced mathematics schemes at their own pace. They followed instructions within the text or queued for guidance from the teacher. In this context personalised learning was at the level of the child learning at the pace they selected. The arrival of the national strategies changed this and personalisation became more focused on structuring learning to ability groups. The strategies and frameworks have given teachers a new range of technical and technological skills. However, it is essential to move even further. With the information we now have about the brain it is time to take thinking about personalisation in the classroom to a new level.

It is essential that the classroom is seen as a community where we:

- Build friendships and affiliations
- Create a community agenda where teachers and pupils plan the intentional learning
- Create community activities for learning though dialogue, reciprocal teaching and group goals for assessment
- Allow group governance so that all partners can create the classroom they want
- Provide a community climate of trust and positive behaviour where all children are ready to learn and to help others learn

When classrooms operate as genuine communities:

- People feel part of a much larger whole
- Diverse contributions are encouraged and celebrated
- Engaged community enquiry emerges
- Students learn as much from each other as they do from the teacher
- There is regular transfer of learning from one area to another
- Children constantly learn how to learn both individually and from each other
- Group and self-discipline develops

The materials provided will allow you to shape a vision for the very best learning environments. As you pursue your vision you will start to match the learning environment to what is known about the development of the human brain. This is essential because as it said at the start of this chapter:

> Without an understanding of what the brain was designed to do in the environment in which we evolved, the unnatural activity called education is unlikely to succeed.

Chapter 6

Creating a Vision for Developing Positive Attitudes to the Social and Emotional Aspects of Learning

I'd like to see us educate the soul and not just the mind. The result would be a person who could live in this world creatively, make good friendships, live in a place he loved, do work that is rewarding, and make a contribution to the community. People say that the word 'educate' means to draw out a person's potential. I like the 'duc' part in the middle of it. To be educated is to become a duke, a leader, a person of stature and colour, a presence and a character.

Thomas Moore in John Gatto, *Dumbing Us Down:*
The Hidden Curriculum of Compulsory Education (2005)

The Prologue

Forgive Me Lord, For I Have Sinned

For several years now I have wondered if Local Authority advisers and Ofsted inspectors are actually the right people to judge teaching and learning. In my early days as a school improvement adviser I had an experience that left me with the view that it might possibly be better left in the hands of the consumers.

The first ever school visit I was required to make was to carry out a review of pupil behaviour and attitudes. My new boss Harold had a reputation of high expectations and a low tolerance of underachievement from all his staff. One head teacher once said that he sounded like God on Judgement Day. He demanded that I should associate with 'challenge' and said that he was looking forward to my perceptive report.

So with increasing trepidation I set off to visit my first school. The instructions were still ringing in my head. I had to know everything about the school and ensure that I fulfilled my role with challenge. Megson Grove Primary School is situated on a post-war housing estate three miles from the town centre. Jobs had been lost in the area following the closure of the steel works and coal mines. Aspiration was low in many households.

Megson Grove Primary School had been described by Ofsted as satisfactory. Previous reports from the local authority had been relatively positive. The school believed it was doing well and celebrated its achievements. In reality this was a typical **outside in school**. It had purchased sets of books from Ginn, Heinemann and Collins to aid teaching and learning within the literacy hour. The teachers were especially pleased with the publisher's photocopiable worksheets. QCA schemes of work were fully incorporated into the curriculum. Many of the children said they were enjoying their study of the Great Fire of London. However, in most lessons teacher talk dominated, and the attention of children drifted which often led to fidgeting and minor disruption. When this occurred teachers became critical of pupils. Children lost privileges or got sent out of the classroom. On one occasion two children sent from the classroom got into further mischief in the cloakrooms out of boredom. It was regularly pointed out when children were misbehaving but there was little praise for children who contributed well within lessons. In short the school curriculum lacked relevance to the children and was unimaginative and bland. It also employed reactive rather than proactive approaches to behaviour and attitudes.

My challenge was either to write about these significant issues in a perceptive report that did not match previous judgements on the school or simply redraft the previous Ofsted and Local Authority reports to promote a more flattering view of the school. To add further pressure the task had to be completed within ten days.

Writer's block struck. Each day brought increased pressure and stress. Each day I started the report, and each day I abandoned the report. It was on day nine that I committed my sin. That evening I was in an Italian restaurant with friends. I had been reluctant to go out because I knew that I should be focusing on the report which was hanging over my head. On the next table was a family of four celebrating a child's birthday. There was Mum, Dad and two daughters aged about 9 and 11. They were enjoying a pleasant evening. However, as the night progressed the children talked more and more about their school, which was—you've guessed it—Megson Grove Primary School.

Their conversation was as systematic and evidence based as an Ofsted inspection team meeting. They discussed the quality of teaching and learning in every classroom and how the children in the class responded to their teachers. They described how a few teachers opened up their minds whilst the majority closed them down. It was as though they had an intuitive understanding of the reptilian brain. One of the children described how certain teachers seemed to create work for the learning mentors. They spoke of classroom organisation, learning environments and behaviour strategies. They described the effects of marking and feedback carried out by different teachers. They knew which teachers were inspirational and which classrooms were dull places. They backed up each judgement with clear evidence. They described the strengths and areas for development. They described their own vision of what the children needed and how they would enjoy their education better in the future. I listened with intrigue and decided to try to memorise their comments.

I went straight home and made myself comfortable at the dining room table. The computer loaded itself up and I commenced the report once more. It was as though the words flowed straight from my fingertips into the keyboard and onto the screen in front of me. Without fully realising it, I was writing an extremely judgemental and controversial report that argued that the school was spending too much time teaching the wrong things. The school urgently needed to reduce subject content and become more proactive in teaching and modelling values. I pressed the submit key on the keyboard and waited in trepidation like a northern Jerry Maguire, but taller.

The wait was not long. The next day I was sitting at my desk. Harold approached and said in a voice that absolutely sounded like the voice of God: 'Megson Grove Primary School. We need to speak about your report as a matter of urgency. Come to my office at 3 p.m. prompt.'

I was now sat before God and it was my Judgement Day. I was a nervous wreck. There was a few seconds delay and the silence was deafening. I knew my first report was a sham. Nervously, I said, 'I am afraid there is something I need to tell you about this report.' However, there was no chance to elaborate. He waved his hand and dismissed my comments saying, 'Later, later my man. I have got to say, Will, this is a damned fine report. It is one of the most perceptive I have ever read and it has come so early in your career. You really have set a high standard to live up to in the future. Now, Will, at the next team meeting you will explain all the strategies you used to collect the evidence for this report. Some of your more experienced colleagues will benefit from your advice.'

I have thought about this experience many times over the years. I believe too many schools are still spending too much time teaching the wrong things. The strange thing is that the schools do too. During training sessions I often ask whether it is knowledge, skills or attitudes that is the most important thing we teach. Time after time the delegates respond that attitudes are the most important followed by skills then knowledge. After this they usually tell me that their current reality places the emphasis on knowledge, then skills and then attitudes. The brave amongst them then recognise and commit to the absolute need for change. They are right because knowledge is available via Google whereas a focus on developing emotional intelligence will help children to develop self-belief, aspiration and success. This chapter aids the process. It helps school leaders to carry out professional development opportunities that will aid them to create a vision for high quality pupil behaviour and attitudes through an investigation of positive behaviour strategies and the key components of emotional intelligence.

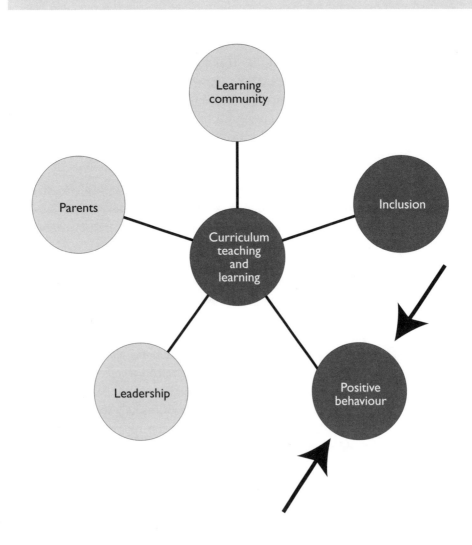

Introduction

Walking in to a primary school can be a magical experience. Anyone can pick up the atmosphere of a school very quickly. Within a few minutes of being there, talking to staff and seeing the pupils at work, you will know about the relationships that exist within the organisation. In our best schools there is a purposeful excitement, a clear sense of purpose and a strong air of calm and order. The ethos is there for all to experience because it is all pervasive and its impact is powerful. Children who are new to setting can quickly pick up on the norms and expectations of the school. Ensuring a positive shared ethos is a high priority to the **inside out school leader** because of its impact on both learning and the wider community. In our best schools there is:

- An expectation on the part of both adults and children that learning is important and enjoyable and that everyone can achieve and help each other to achieve.
- A wide range of teaching approaches and a culture of collaboration within learning.
- Teachers and staff who are ambitious for the children and expectations and aspirations are very high.
- Children who are motivated and believe they can.

The question is how do these magical conditions come about? It certainly isn't through coincidence. Growing up in the twenty-first century is remarkably difficult. Although very few inspection reports on primary schools identify significant issues relating to pupil behaviour, teachers will tell you that children come to schools with increasingly complex needs. The government's own research shows that despite the millions of pounds pumped into education your life chances are still largely determined by where you are born. In some of our local communities, aspiration and expectation are low and children enter school with low self-esteem and underdeveloped social and emotional skills. This affects both attitudes and behaviour.

Many researchers have spoken of the anti-swot culture amongst boys which can be prevalent by the time the child enters Key Stage 2. Some argue that this culture comes from an overcrowded curriculum, the teaching styles used in some classrooms, the systems for praise and reward, the length of tasks given to pupils and the importance given to academic success. Others say it is simpler than that and boils down to the fact that boys see themselves as different to girls—and girls enjoy school and do well there. In some schools this can lead to an '8:8' culture (age 8 to year 8) where boys do not get their 'street cred' from behaving and doing well. Elsewhere other schools cope with the realities of growing up in the twenty-first century really well and create a positive work ethic that all children sign up to. This occurs when behaviour is taught and not simply caught.

The government has now recognised the need to teach positive behaviour and self-esteem through the production of the excellent Social and Emotional Aspects of Learning (SEAL) resource published by the Primary National Strategy. In 2003 the rise in attainment had hit a plateau and the government believed that a focus on explicitly teaching social, emotional and behavioural skills would help results to rise once more. Where children are taught the appropriate skills of emotional literacy, emotional intelligence, and social and emotional competence—and when they are educated in an environment supportive of their holistic health and well-being—they will:

- Become successful learners
- Make and sustain friendships
- Deal with and resolve conflicts effectively and fairly
- Solve problems with others or by themselves
- Manage strong feelings such as anger, anxiety or frustration
- Recover from setbacks and persist in the face of difficulties
- Work and play cooperatively
- Compete fairly and lose with dignity and respect other competitors

This chapter helps you to create a vision that will allow this to happen. There will be a clear focus on two strands: developing and embedding strategies for positive attitudes and behaviour at a whole school level, and teaching emotional intelligence.

Teaching and embedding strategies for positive attitudes and behaviour at a whole school level

The first challenge for the **inside out school leader** is to embed the teaching of positive behaviour into the fabric of teaching and learning within the school. For this to happen schools and teachers must be convinced that they can make a difference to pupil behaviour and attitudes, some of which stem from the home and community. This can be a challenge because for every hour in a child's life they spend nine minutes in school and fifty-one minutes elsewhere. However, that could lead to the assumption that issues relating to positive behaviour and attitudes only stem from the home and locality. When the Elton Report into school discipline was published twenty years ago they found that eighty per cent of poor behaviour in school was due to poor teaching in classrooms rather than other factors. The report clearly stressed the role of schools and teachers:

> The teacher, as leader in the classroom, must ensure high and achievable expectations for both learning and behaviour. Pupils are expected to behave according to convention but may not have been taught the skills required to do this. It is proper that teachers should have high expectations of pupil behaviour but this requires that procedures and structures are put in place for teaching pupils how to live up to these expectations. Teaching strategies and techniques that promote positive behaviour are only effective if they are manageable within the classroom setting and thus it is essential that they are integrated into the fabric of teaching and learning.
>
> Discipline in Schools: Report of the Committee of Enquiry Chaired by Lord Elton (1989)

In **inside out schools** all staff *genuinely* subscribe to *and believe* the following principles:

- High quality teaching promotes high quality attitudes and behaviour.
- The way that pupils feel about a learning environment affects the way that they behave.
- It is possible to establish teaching and learning environments that promote appropriate behaviour and positive relationships.
- Positive behaviour stems from positive relationships, explicit and taught expectations and effective communication.
- Pupils can change their behaviour if the right structure and support is put in place.
- The whole school community has a role to play in supporting pupils as they strive to change and manage their behaviour.
- Whole school systems of support promote consistency and increase teacher confidence in managing pupil behaviour.
- Improved behaviour can be sustained by regular reviewing of school and classroom positive behaviour management strategies.

In short, developing high standards in behaviour cannot be left to chance. For decades initial teacher training has paid insufficient attention to this area of work, leaving teachers either poorly skilled or working by instinct (some of which has been highly successful but on other occasions it has led to a downward spiral in behaviour). Once these conditions have been established staff need to understand and apply the following principles if they are to be equipped to teach positive behaviour.

- Teachers and staff must use the concept of what has become known as the 4Rs Framework (rights, responsibilities, rules and routines) and how it fits into classroom behaviour planning. Rights and responsibilities are inextricably linked and are the basis on which classroom relationships, teaching and learning are built. All members of the school community have rights and responsibilities. Rules are the mechanism by which rights and responsibilities are translated into adult and pupil behaviours. Routines underpin rules and reinforce classroom order. A classroom behaviour plan is the process through which the teacher teaches the 4Rs Framework. All teachers know how they would like pupils to behave in their classrooms but not all teachers have a clear structure for their behaviour management.

- There is a difference between teaching positive behaviour and managing classroom behaviour. For many pupils good behaviour and positive attitudes have to be learned. This means it requires teaching the same as any other subject on the curriculum. This has to be followed by opportunities for regular practice. The four components of a successful behaviour plan are rules, routines, positive recognition and negative consequences.

- All staff have a role in promoting positive behaviour and establishing a positive learning environment in which teachers can teach and pupils can learn. In such an environment positive behaviour and attitudes and appropriate values are modelled persistently. In these classrooms positivity and the creation of highly effective relationships abound. In short teachers teach respect by modelling respect.

> Children must grow up in an environment that stresses self-motivation and assessment. Schools that focus on external motivating factors such as rewards and punishments and meeting goals set by others are denying children the tools they need most to survive... As the world moves toward universal recognition of individual rights within a democratic society people must be empowered to participate as equal partners.
>
> David Albert in John Gatto, *Dumbing Us Down: The Hidden Curriculum of Compulsory Education* (2005)

- The language of choice has to be used by teachers to help pupils recognise that actions have consequences. In school, as in all other areas of life, the choices we make cannot be separated from the consequences that follow. The 'night follows day' principle must be consistently applied in classrooms.

- Incentive systems are extremely important and they are most effective when behaviour objectives are identified and reinforced at the beginning of each session, expected behaviour is taught and rehearsed, targets are clearly displayed and referred to, feedback on behaviour is given at the end of each session and they incorporate social approval and acknowledge success.

- When giving directions to pupils it is essential that staff describe what they want them to 'do' rather than what they want them to 'stop doing'. Reframing language from 'don't' to 'do' is important because it accurately describes the desired outcome, is clear and unequivocal and provides an alternative course of action for the pupils.

The following exercise will help you to develop a vision for what you need to do next in order to develop positive behaviour and attitudes within your school. The left-hand column lists the prompts. In the right-hand column grade your response using the following scale: (1) fully in place in all classrooms, parts of the school and for all staff, (2) some areas for development still exist, and (3) overall area of weakness.

Establishing and embedding positive behaviour and attitudes	Grade
Do **all** staff have consistently high expectations with regard to behaviour?	
Do **all** staff follow behaviour management plans for identified pupils?	
Do **all** staff work within and actively teach your 4Rs Framework?	
Do **all** staff model the behaviours that they wish to see?	
Do **all** staff discipline with dignity and correct with compassion?	
Do **all** staff consistently use the language of choice?	
Do **all** staff focus on promoting appropriate values in pupils?	
Do **all** staff actively build trust with pupils?	
Do **all** staff look for opportunities to catch pupils being good?	
Do **all** staff follow up/through with rewards and sanctions?	
Do **all** staff actively take steps to reduce confrontation?	

Establishing and embedding positive behaviour and attitudes (*contd*)	Grade
Do **all** staff actively develop and use a range of intervention strategies?	
Do **all** staff ensure that consequences are fair and logical?	
Now describe your vision for high quality pupil attitudes and behaviour in three years' time.	
PLANS What will be different in one year's time?	

Developing emotional intelligence

It has been claimed that a person's life chances of success are eighty per cent dependent on emotional intelligence rather than their IQ. The person with a high emotional intelligence knows and understands themself well and has a strong self-confidence. They also have the capacity to form positive relationships with others. The need for schools to come to grips with teaching emotional intelligence is now essential. Research shows that one in ten children between the ages of 1 and 15 has mental health problems. The United Kingdom has one of the highest rates of self-harm in Europe and a 2007 Unicef report showed that British schoolchildren were amongst the unhappiest in the industrialised world (source: Unicef, *Child Poverty in Perspective: An Overview of Child Well-being in Rich Countries* (2007); Department for Health, *National Service Framework for Mental Health—Five Years On* (2005)).

The concept of emotional intelligence has been extensively researched by Daniel Goleman. A focus on teaching emotional intelligence in the primary school and creating the appropriate supporting conditions will make children thrive because it impacts on how children behave as learners. Children's difficulties in learning can be caused by such things as demotivation, fear of failure and the impact of managing feelings and behaviour rather than a lack of ability. In *Emotional Intelligence* (1997) Goleman argues that to overcome these barriers there needs to be a clear focus on self-awareness, managing feelings, motivation, empathy and social skills.

Self-awareness

Self-awareness is a key factor in becoming a successful learner and is at the centre of social and emotional well-being. Schools that teach self-awareness are:

- Helping children to make sense of what they think and feel
- Providing pupils with the skills to manage, organise and direct their thinking, feelings and learning
- Supporting pupil progress and attainment

The child who is self-aware understands that:

- Feelings, thoughts and behaviours are different things
- Feelings vary in intensity
- Feelings are acceptable *but not all behaviours are acceptable*
- The context affects the acceptability of behaviours
- We can have conflicting feelings and these affect our behaviours
- Our thoughts affect our behaviours
- There is a need to talk about our feelings to develop shared understanding
- They should recognise a feeling in themselves from internal and external cues

Self-awareness is especially important in planning and decision making. Effective learners can plan their learning and consider the resources they may need and the obstacles they might meet. They understand and can speak about the way in which they learn best within a particular circumstance. High quality assessment for learning opportunities is significant in developing pupil self-awareness.

The following exercise will help you to develop a vision for what you need to do next in order to develop self-awareness within your school. The left-hand column lists the prompts. In the right-hand column grade your response using the following scale: (1) fully in place in all classrooms, parts of the school and for all staff, (2) some areas for development still exist, and (3) overall area of weakness.

Promoting self-awareness	Grade
The pupils in our school have high levels of self-awareness	
Children are provided with formative assessment of their learning progress and future needs	
Children receive regular feedback on their behaviour	
Children receive opportunities to express personal choice	
Classrooms are emotionally safe places where children talk about thoughts and feelings	
Opportunities also exist to discuss pupils' and others' feelings, mood and emotions	
Children discuss and form personal values	
Children reflect on their own learning and behaviour and its impact on others	
Children evaluate their own skills and abilities in working with others	
Children have opportunities to identify their own success criteria	
Children plan how to use their time and resources	
Children mentor and support the learning of others	
Children are aware of and help to set their personal goals	
Children can predict what they will do well and the areas of learning where they will experience difficulties	
Children recognise their own achievements, strengths and weaknesses	
Children reflect on their and others' learning styles and strategies for working	
Children review and evaluate what they and others have done	

 Now describe how the situation will be different in three years' time (you could list the key improvements that will be made).

 What will be different in one year's time (list your key actions)?

Self-awareness makes it possible for children to manage their feelings. Without self-awareness children are more likely to be impulsive, lash out in anger or be selfish without considering what the consequences might be. Self-awareness allows people to recognise how they are feeling, allowing them to pause and weigh up the situation and manage their feelings more effectively.

Managing feelings

Managing feelings or self-regulation has a direct link to behaviour, thus impacting on the conditions for learning in the classroom. It is important to recognise at this stage that where a teacher does not promote supportive conditions for learning, or the ethos is weak, it will create negative emotions in the child which they will find difficult to manage.

Managing feelings is integral to effective learning. Pupils in schools and classrooms will experience a range of experiences. Hopefully many of the feelings will be positive such as absorption in work, satisfaction in a well-completed task and pride from praise. However, there is also exposure to negative and unpleasant feelings such as frustration, confusion, disappointment and fear. Children with fragile self-esteem will be especially vulnerable to this latter set of feelings. School bells and session times can be an immense frustration to some pupils who feel that just as they are getting into a task they have to stop and move on to a new activity and this brings frustration. Within **inside out schools** there is a clear understanding about the significance of negative emotions. The staff are aware that:

- Feelings build up over time and therefore small irritations can suddenly lead to a significant overreaction.
- Emotional memory is very powerful. If a pupil has had a powerful emotional experience, an unrelated sight, sound or smell that links to this experience could trigger negative emotions.
- When pupils experience a strong negative emotion such as anger or fear it takes a long time for their emotional temperature to cool. During this time it is easy for a child to feel the same emotion again.
- Emotions are triggered very quickly and rational thought is triggered more slowly. This potentially leads to inappropriate actions.

The best learning takes place where the challenge is high but appropriate. This means that it is essential to build up a child's resilience and a desire to push them forward into the challenge. Children need to trust their self-awareness about when to persist and equally when to take a break. In doing this they are developing themselves as independent learners. As a consequence teachers need to know when to intervene with children, when to resist the impulse to drive the child on and when to refrain from moving children to another task.

The following exercise will help you to develop a vision for what you need to do next in order to develop pupils' capacity to mange their feelings within your school. The left-hand column lists the prompts. In the right-hand column grade your response using the following scale: (1) fully in place in all classrooms, parts of the school and for all staff, (2) some areas for development still exist, and (3) overall area of weakness.

Managing feelings	Grade
The pupils in our school have high levels of skills in managing their feelings	
Children know when to seek support and where to find it in order to manage their feelings	
Children are taught calming down strategies	
Children are given opportunities to identify feelings and situations they find difficult to manage	
Children know when these feelings arise most strongly	
Children learn how to express and deal with them	
Children learn about the consequences of the way in which they deal with them	
Children learn about effective ways of expressing feelings	
Children know what distracts them and prevents them from being an effective learner	

 Now describe how the situation will be different in three years' time (you could list the key improvements that will be made).

 What will be different in one year's time (list your key actions)?

Motivation

Intrinsic motivation involves knowing what you want to achieve and being willing to pursue these goals even when difficulties occur. Developing the habits of self-motivation is an essential ingredient of learning to learn. Primary practitioners need to build this capacity within children. If children are to become better at learning, they have to want to learn. This means that they see the importance of learning to learn. Pupils need to develop independence in which they set and work towards their own learning goals thus developing a range of study skills along the way. Intrinsic motivation encompasses mature emotional and sometimes social behaviour. This is because the gratification for reaching the goal is often in the future rather than the here and now. Pupils who are intrinsically motivated are able to work towards longer term personal goals or see activities as worthwhile in their own right.

For some pupils delaying gratification can be a challenge and for such pupils external reward structures such as special mentions, stickers and notes home are significant support.

The following exercise will help you to develop a vision for what you need to do next in order to develop motivation within your school. The left hand column lists the prompts. In the right hand column grade your response using the following scale: (1) fully in place in all classrooms, parts of the school and for all staff, (2) some areas for development still exist, and (3) overall area of weakness.

Motivation	Grade
The pupils in our school have a high level of intrinsic motivation	
Children are regularly exposed to biographies of individuals from diverse social, cultural, ethnic and gender backgrounds who have overcome great difficulties to achieve a goal	
Children are encouraged to discuss projects they would like to carry out but never get round to, so that the reasons are analysed	
The school invites visitors into school who have a specific skill but can discuss how they worked to learn that skill	
Teachers and others demonstrate to others that they are learners and that they need to persevere	

Motivation (continued)	Grade
Classes in school have the opportunity to identify the things that they would like to learn about and have the opportunities to do so	
Individual pupils are given opportunities to pursue or initiate their own learning which the adults sensitively support	

 Now describe how the situation will be different in three years' time (you could list the key improvements that will be made).

 What will be different in one year's time (list your key actions)?

Empathy

Pupils with empathy have the ability to enrich communication and perception by looking at the world from different perspectives. The youngest children look at the world largely from their own viewpoint. However, most children rapidly move on to build models in their mind about how things look and feel to others. Empathy impacts on children's lives in schools because it enables children to work and play with each other and it plays a significant role in helping pupils to build relationships. Good teachers have regularly used empathy in role play situations or hot seating as part of a history study. However, the effective teaching of empathy can lead to an essential life skill. Neuroscientists have found that our brains are designed to imitate others, and this tendency enables children first of all to simply copy others but then to internalise the ways of talking, arguing, remembering and thinking of older or more experienced people. If a young child is encouraged to work with good role models, or selects to do so, they will expand their repertoire of positive learning skills.

The following exercise will help you to develop a vision for what you need to do next in order to develop motivation within your school. The left-hand column lists the prompts. In the right-hand column grade your response using the following scale: (1) fully in place in all classrooms, parts of the school and for all staff, (2) some areas for development still exist, and (3) overall area of weakness.

Empathy	Grade
The pupils in our school have high levels of empathy with other individuals and groups	
Our pupils respect each other, support each other and are tolerant of each other	
Children regularly develop empathy throughout the curriculum. This could include role play, conscience alleys and discussion activities which allow them to think about issues through the viewpoint of others	
Regular opportunities are provided for children to explore traits such as kindness, generosity, thoughtfulness and scruffiness in order to develop positive images and prevent pupils jumping to conclusions	
Children take part in reflective discussions and have an awareness of the different groups that make up our society	
Children are given opportunities to work with others who are good role models	
Children are involved in projects to ensure that all pupils feel included in the life of the school (e.g. Does the playground meet the needs of all pupils? How could the classroom be made better for a disabled child?)	

Now describe the situation in three years' time (you could list the key improvements that will be made).

 What will be different in one year's time (list your key actions)?

Social skills

Clearly many children pick up social skills almost without thinking. Young children are curious and are keen to join the society around them. However, our society is rapidly changing and children need to be able to function well in a diverse cultural world. Schools need to be able to work with children, parents, carers and the local community to prevent cultural clashes arising. In the school situation children need to be supported to learn more complex social interactions. Sometimes this involves unlearning or overriding previous learning. Children need to learn and be coached in acceptable social behaviour. Educational achievement will be jeopardised if this does not happen. Schools therefore need to pay explicit attention to the teaching of emotional skills, recognising that it enhances emotional well-being and allows pupils to interact purposefully with others. The following exercise will help you to develop a vision for what you need to do next in order to develop social skills within your school. The left-hand column lists the prompts. In the right-hand column grade your response using the following scale: (1) fully in place in all classrooms, parts of the school and for all staff, (2) some areas for development still exist, and (3) overall area of weakness.

Developing social skills	Grade
Children are given opportunities to share information and ideas together and can do this successfully	
Children are given effective discussions and as a consequence they know when to talk and when to listen	
Children are given opportunities to both join a group and lead a group or team so that they can use their strengths and support others	
Children learn to give feedback well and give it to others in a supportive manner	
Children take part in reflective discussions about their work and if necessary change direction	
Children regularly choose the right people to learn with and from	
Children are given opportunities and know the rules of argument and debate	
In these situations children have the courage and skill to defend a minority opinion	
Children are taught how to resolve conflict	
Children are able to apologise with sincerity	
Children know how to take turns fairly	

Now describe how the situation will be different in three years' time (you could list the key improvements that will be made).

 What will be different in one year's time (list your key actions)?

Summary

Schools come under considerable pressure to raise standards and seek quick-fix solutions that will add a further one or two per cent to the results. However, it is important that they see the big picture and focus on the whole child. The need to develop good behaviour, positive attitudes and emotional intelligence is paramount.

> Our evidence suggests that many children who behave badly in school are those whose self-esteem is threatened by failure. They see academic work as competitive and the competition as unwinnable. They soon realise that the best way to avoid failure in such a competition is not to enter it.
>
> *Discipline in Schools: Report of the Committee of Enquiry Chaired by*
> *Lord Elton* (1989)

Creating a Vision for Developing Positive Attitudes

This chapter opened with a suggestion that walking in to a primary school can be a magical experience. **Inside out schools** achieve this because they put the following conditions in place:

- There is an ethos built on the belief that everyone is valued and should be understood.
- There is recognition by pupils that staff treat them fairly and are committed to teaching them.
- There are effective and consistent routines, such as the way pupils move round school and the way lessons begin and end.
- Pupils feel secure in terms of the physical environment and are being taught to be emotionally intelligent.
- Learning is dynamic, interesting and challenging and delivered through a curriculum that meets the needs of the school community.
- There is a clear partnership between school, pupils and parents.
- There is constant celebration of success.

Inside out school leaders believe that if you educate the soul and not just the mind:

> The result would be a person who could live in this world creatively, make good friendships, live in a place he loved, do work that is rewarding, and make a contribution to the community. People say that the word educate means to draw out a person's potential. I like the 'duc' part in the middle of it. To be educated is to become a duke, a leader, a person of stature and colour, a presence and a character.
>
> Thomas Moore in John Gatto, *Dumbing Us Down: The Hidden Curriculum of Compulsory Education* (2005)

Chapter 7

Creating a Vision for Inclusion

People who say it cannot be done should not interfere with those who are doing it.

Anon.

The Prologue

Thomas

'Oy, give me my lollipop back!' screamed Mrs Barton as she set off in hot pursuit of Thomas as he raced up the busy lane. Thomas was a fit 10 year old who was now hurtling away brandishing the fluorescent pole saying 'STOP—CHILDREN CROSSING'. Other children and their parents ducked for cover as the lollipop was waved vigorously from side to side. Mrs Barton, who had a heart of gold and had patrolled the crossing for twenty-five years, gave good chase. Children leaned over the school fence urging their favourite lollipop lady to find extra pace; others chanted her name as the race picked up further speed. In reality, there was only ever going to be one winner. Thomas's younger years and Nike trainers were always going to be a greater asset than Mrs Barton's bright yellow heavy waterproof coat and furry boots. Once Thomas had gained sufficient ground he turned round and shouted a four-letter expletive and tossed the crossing lady's lollipop over a garden fence where it came to rest in a pond next to two garden gnomes and a sign saying 'Gone fishing'. Mrs Barton hitched up her coat, climbed over the fence and retrieved her pole, which had served her for twenty-five years. Every year at Christmas she had decorated it with tinsel and fairy lights and she was darned if she was going to lose it now.

Ten minutes earlier I had been sitting with Thomas and his mother discussing 'What next?', because his problems and behaviour were starting to spiral out of control and he was causing deep concern. We retraced the events of the past year since Thomas had joined the school. Thomas came to us late in Year 5 when he had moved into the area with his older brother who had become addicted to drugs. In order to fund the addiction he stole from his mother and sold many of Thomas's possessions. The house was frequently trashed. Thomas did not find school work easy and he found building relationships even harder. He knew that it would never be possible to invite a potential friend round to the house to play because there was nothing to play with, nor was it a home that he could be proud to entertain in. The other families were wary anyway and parents regarded Thomas as bad news. Thomas therefore couldn't make the friendships he was desperate for. Each time a new child or family joined the school he sought friendship; sometimes he would steal money to buy the newcomer presents but it never worked. As a consequence Thomas became more and more aggressive and he was very good at fighting.

Serious problems had developed over recent weeks and they were rapidly escalating. It was summertime and the days were longer. It was light well into the evening and Thomas had started hanging around with a group of youths who were much older than him. In reality this group were using Thomas as a plaything. They were ridiculing him and having a good laugh at his expense. However, to Thomas any company was better than no company, and he could make them laugh and that made him feel good. However, before long alcohol and drugs were introduced to Thomas and at that point the decline became rapid.

On one particular evening Thomas passed out after being given a cocktail of strong lager and a cannabis cake. The group he was with shaved his head and tied him to a lamp post. Whilst Thomas felt stupid the next day he was praised by his new 'mates' for being such a 'good laugh'. That was all he needed to be hooked on their company. At last he considered that he had friends and that gave him some form of self-esteem. Before long the group were using him to hide drugs and to steal alcohol from a local supermarket.

The situation was rapidly deteriorating in school. Stories of Thomas's evening escapades were starting to circulate and this was making him even more aggressive. Violence towards and theft from other pupils was now prevalent and after a series of incidents I decided to exclude Thomas for a short fixed term. It seemed that the other children needed a break from Thomas and it didn't seem fair to keep bringing him into an environment where he was constantly failing. Whether or not this was the right decision or not, I still do not know. However, a week where his mother could focus totally on Thomas seemed like a good idea.

Half way through the week's exclusion Thomas appeared in school, even though this was strictly forbidden under the regulations. However he knew when and where he could find me alone. He told me he had some drugs hidden at the home of one of his teenage accomplices and that he wanted me to go with him to destroy them so he would not be tempted into further trouble. I briefly told the deputy head what was going on and where I was going. I was feeling sort of brave about it until she said, 'You do know they shot someone up there last week?'

I parked outside the house. Thomas made up a story that he had left his home-work there and that we had come to collect it. He entered the house and returned a few minutes later with a supermarket carrier bag containing his stash of illegal goods. He handed them over and pleaded with me not to tell the police. Rightly or wrongly I didn't. The deputy head witnessed me destroy the drugs.

And so the story moved on to the infamous Monday morning of the great lolli-pop theft. Thomas had arrived in school with his mother to discuss his return to the classroom. I deliberately asked them to come early so that Thomas could be reintegrated back into his class with all the other pupils at 9 a.m. Together the three of us drew up a programme of support and things seemed to be going well until near the end of this conversation Thomas's mother asked him why he was wearing so many clothes. True enough, when you looked closely he was actually wearing three jumpers and underneath his trousers were a pair of tracksuit bot-toms. He simply said he felt cold when he got up. In reality he was preparing to run away from home.

As our conversation concluded Thomas said he wanted to go to his classroom before the other children arrived. He walked though the hall. He smiled and waved at his teacher who said that he was pleased to see him back in school. But Thomas just kept on walking straight out of the school gate and towards the school crossing. As he left the kerb Mrs Barton said, 'Thomas, you are going the wrong way.' That proved to be the straw that broke Thomas's back. He grabbed the lollipop and went careering up the road with Mrs Barton in glorious pursuit.

That was the last I saw of Thomas for a while. A few weeks later I went to see him in a secure home for troubled and vulnerable youngsters which was operated by the Local Authority. He seemed pleased to see me and was clearly trying to make amends. Shortly afterwards he left the area and I am left still wondering.

As I look back I do not know which bits I got right and which bits I got wrong. Some people say I should have given up on him at an earlier stage. Personally I don't think that I have given up on him now and ten years have passed. Amongst all the confusion that I still feel, there are certain things that I do know. Thomas was not born bad. It was other things that drove to him to low self-esteem and in the end crime. Often in our schools inclusion comes at a tremendous cost but non-inclusion is even more costly.

This chapter provides a clear principled rationale for inclusion. It helps you identify those pupils who may be missing out in your school through a checklist of pupil inclusion indicators. It urges schools to seek creative solutions to break down the barriers to the learning process for these pupils. The text provides a clear view of what our most inclusive schools look like and provides a reality check which will help you to shape your vision for the future.

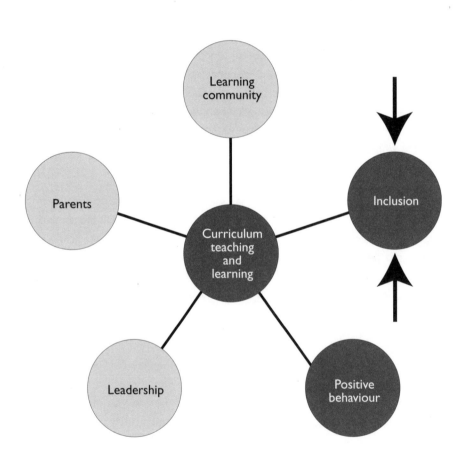

Introduction

On the day I sat down to write this chapter the Sutton Trust published a report into social disadvantage. It concluded that social mobility in the UK remains at the low level it was for those born in 1970, with recent generations of children's educational outcomes still overwhelmingly tied to their parents' income. The research was backed by depressing statistics including:

- Those from the poorest fifth of households but in the brightest group drop from the eighty-eighth percentile on cognitive tests at age 3 to the sixty-fifth percentile at age 5. Those from the richest households who are least able at age 3 move up from the fifteenth percentile to the forty-fifth percentile by age 5. If this trend were to continue, the children from affluent backgrounds would be likely to overtake the poorer children in test scores by age 7.

- Inequalities in obtaining a degree persist across different income groups. While forty-four per cent of young people from the richest twenty per cent of households acquired a degree in 2002, only ten per cent from the poorest twenty per cent of households did so (source: Jo Blanden and Stephen Machin, *Recent Changes in Intergenerational Mobility in Britain* (2007)).

In short too many children and groups of children fail to do well enough because they do not feel included in our educational system. Within education the word inclusion can be controversial. Some relate it to special needs provision, others to the removal of special schools and some to cost. **Inside out schools** regard it as a moral purpose because they believe that education makes a powerful contribution to the social construction of inclusive communities in an inclusive society. Inclusive education is concerned with the human right for children to receive increased opportunity to engage in lifelong learning and employment through access to, and participation in, an appropriate mainstream community based education.

Sadly many **outside in schools** see inclusion as a threat. Teachers will say things like:

> How can I possibly get through all the learning outcomes prescribed by the government in a challenging and fast paced manner and at the same time provide appropriate challenge for those on the special educational needs register?

If inclusion relates to human rights, and I have a pupil who constantly disrupts the learning of others, do the rights of one pupil come above the rights of the majority?

Can a mainstream school really support children with complex needs?

Isn't it better for skilful teaching assistants to withdraw pupils rather than leave them to struggle in the classroom?

In reality there are a host of other questions which regularly get asked and which are equally difficult to answer. There is clear evidence that some schools are fearful of admitting pupils with special educational needs or pupils who speak English as an additional language because they consider results will fall. Equally some schools consider that they do not have the appropriate financial or human resources to support certain children. However non-inclusive approaches are extremely dangerous because:

- They result in lower expectations because there is an acceptance that academic and social learning outcomes are limited for some pupils by virtue of a child's genetic inheritance and/or social circumstances.
- By segregating vulnerable pupils from mainstream and community activities there is a lost opportunity for all children to experience the benefits of learning and socialising with a range of different individuals.
- It promotes the notion that difference or diversity from the 'norm' is something that has to be pitied and provided for through a separate framework rather than celebrated or understood.

For this reason the best **inside out schools** make a commitment to:

- Systematically monitor the progress each pupil makes. ✴
- Identify individuals or groups who may be missing out, difficult to engage or in some way missing out.✴
- Take all practical steps to meet each pupil's needs effectively and remove barriers to the learning process.
- Develop caring, tolerant and understanding participants in a diverse society. ✴

The reason for this is that they believe in:

- Valuing all students and staff equally.
- Creating better life chances that are created through increasing the participation of children in the cultures, curricula and communities of local schools.
- Developing policies and practices in schools that respond to and meet the needs of the diversity of students in the locality.
- Reducing and removing barriers to learning and creating participation for all students—not only those with impairments or those who are categorised as having special educational needs.
- Viewing the differences between children as being a strength to celebrate and a resource to support learning, rather than as problem to be overcome.
- Acknowledging the right of children and their families to receive an education in their locality.
- Emphasising the role of the school in building communities and developing values, as well as in increasing achievement.
- Fostering mutually sustaining relationships between schools and communities.
- Recognising that inclusion in education can lead to inclusion in society.

What are the indicators that a child feels fully included in the classroom and the life of a school?

Within any classroom there will be particular children who stand out. There will be those with particular special educational needs who may receive direct support or be engaged with an intervention programme. There will be high flying children whose attributes are clearly obvious. However there may be many relatively quiet and possibly hard working children of whom we know very little. There could well be bright children who don't stand out. These children may or may not feel happy and included within school life. They may or may not be working to their full potential.

Inside out schools do not take educational inclusion for granted. They constantly monitor and evaluate the progress each pupil makes. They identify the pupils or groups of pupils who may be missing out, difficult to engage or in some way not participating in what the school seeks to provide. Some of the information school leaders require will come from effective pupil tracking systems relating to National Curriculum levels. However, because **inside out schools** seek to take every practical step in the classroom and beyond to meet pupils' needs effectively, and to promote tolerance and understanding in a diverse society, a range of information is needed. This is achieved through the use of pupil inclusion indicators which give a more holistic view of whether children are experiencing barriers to learning. The set of indicators below could be used in a variety of ways.

- The indicators could be used as a checklist for specific pupils who are not making appropriate progress or children you are concerned about. Having used the checklist it can then be utilised to devise an appropriate and innovative programme of support. Similar checklists have been used by learning mentors or those in similar roles to identify which pupils they should work with and what kind of support should be delivered. Many of the barriers to learning experienced by pupils have been around for a long time. This is because schools have a track record of doing what they have always done and therefore getting what they always got, thus leaving the problem unresolved. **Inside out schools** seek new and innovative solutions.

- The indicators could be used on all pupils. This would usefully ensure that a considerable amount of additional information is known about each child. Too often schools only store assessment information relating to National Curriculum levels. The indicators could be used as a scaffold to detailed conversations about each child between school leaders and class teachers or between class teachers and their teaching assistants. They could also be highly informative for reporting to parents.

- If the inclusion indicators are used on all children, or a representative sample of pupils, they will give you a view on how inclusive the school is and any worrying trends relating to vulnerable groups.

Schools will need to determine for themselves how to collect the information. In reality it will be through a variety of strategies including pupil interviews, parental discussions, observations and work scrutiny.

Indicators relating to attendance and family participation

Inclusion is clearly aided by regular, punctual and hopefully enthusiastic attendance patterns that are backed by strong formal and informal support from parents and carers. Positive responses to the following questions would indicate a high level of inclusion. Negative answers could indicate a barrier to the learning process.

- Does the child attend regularly?
- Does the child attend willingly?
- Does the child attend punctually?
- Does the child attend a school in the locality?
- Does the school enjoy good informal links with the family?
- Do parents attend all the appropriate meetings?

Indicators relating to vulnerable groups and cultural links

Every child belongs to some kind of group or groups with whom they feel a sense of identity. It can be as simple as boys or girls. Other groups that can exist within a school include: minority ethnic groups including travellers, asylum seekers and refugees; pupils who speak English as an additional language; pupils who have special educational needs; pupils who are gifted and talented; children in public care; children who are young carers; children from families under stress; and pupils at risk of disaffection.

Clearly children can be in more than one of these groups and the child will cease to feel included if that group is not positively represented within a school community or has become associated with underachievement. Britain has been a multicultural nation since the Romans arrived two hundred years ago. Everyone, including white indigenous Protestants, has an ethnicity relating to culture, regionality and religion. It is important that all children feel they have equal access and inclusion through both the formal and hidden curriculum of the school. Positive responses to the questions below would indicate a higher level of inclusion. Negative answers could indicate a barrier to the learning process.

- Does the child belong to a group or groups that achieves well in the school?
- Does the child belong to a group or groups that are positively represented in school?
- Does the child immediately recognise his or her appropriate role models?
- Does the child have regular access to resources that portray his or her group in a positive light?

Indicators relating to peer relationships and adult relationships

For a child to feel fully included in the life of a school or classroom they need to build and enjoy positive relationships with both adults and their peers. The capacity to form relationships is a key element of building a strong emotional intelligence which can bring success in life. Positive responses to the following questions would indicate a high level of inclusion. Negative answers could indicate a barrier to the learning process.

- Does the child enjoy effective communication with peers?
- Can the child build relationships?
- Can the child deal with conflict?
- Is the pupil fully accepted by the class?
- Does the child have a regular group of friends?
- Is the child regularly accepted by others as a work partner?
- Does the child regularly demonstrate the appropriate social behaviour?
- Is the child safe from bullying, disparagement or peer aggression?

Indicators relating to learning activities and school engagement

For a child to achieve and feel included they need to be able to engage well with classroom and school practice and get enjoyment from their work. A positive response to the following prompts would indicate a high level of inclusion. A negative response would indicate concern.

- Does the child comply well with basic routines?
- Does the child have a range of effective learning habits?
- Does the child complete his or her differentiated work well?
- Does the child enjoy full participation in group work?
- Does the child demonstrate enjoyment, pride and perseverance within their work?
- Is there evidence that the child regularly contributes to full class discussion or question and answer sessions?
- Is there appropriate participation in physical education lessons and physical activity?
- Is the child making appropriate progress in school within literacy and numeracy?
- Is the child making appropriate progress in the other subjects and skills of the National Curriculum?
- Is there appropriate involvement in extracurricular activities?

- Is the child fully involved in educational visits and outings?
- Does the child take part in any decision making activities relating to the school?
- Does the child regularly speak positively about school life?

Indicators relating to self-esteem and emotional security

During training sessions I often ask course members to consider the pupils they are serving and the community in which the children grow up, and then identify an element of their work that is absolutely essential. The most frequent suggestion is to develop the self-esteem of pupils. Children who are self-confident will have the capacity to overcome the challenges and conflicts ahead. Positive responses to the following questions would indicate a high level of inclusion. Negative answers could indicate a lack of self-esteem and emotional security and therefore provide a barrier to the learning process.

- Does the child achieve regular success at home and school?
- Is there evidence of appropriate positive feedback both at home and school?
- Is there evidence of appropriate positive feedback from other children in the class?
- Does the child have obvious hobbies and interests?
- Can the child make the appropriate choices?
- Does the child feel valued?
- Can the child successfully manage moods?
- Is there a freedom from anxiety and anger?
- Is there a freedom from feeling intimidated?

Indicators relating to physical safety

Finally the child needs to feel physically safe within the school. Positive responses to the following questions would indicate a high level of inclusion. Negative answers could indicate a barrier to the learning process.

- Is the child free from minor injuries in the home or school?
- Does the child demonstrate a freedom from impulsive risk?
- Is the child safe from peer aggression in the home or school?
- Is the child safe from adult aggression in the home or school?

Many schools who have learning mentors funded through the Excellence in Cities programme have used pupil indicators to identify which pupils are experiencing barriers to learning and to establish what kind of support should be offered. As a consequence I am aware of learning mentors who:

- Operate walking buses for those who have problems getting to school regularly and on time
- Run homework clubs for those who have difficulties in completing their work at home
- Run ICT activities to support boys who are experiencing difficulties with reading
- Use board games to develop social skills and turn taking
- Provide time-out drop-in centres for those children who struggle with anger management
- Support parents in developing parenting skills
- Operate family learning sessions where parent and child learn together

What do our best inside out schools look like?

An educationally inclusive school is one in which the teaching and learning achievements and attitudes and well-being of every young person matter. All our best schools are educationally inclusive schools. This shows not only in their performance but also in their ethos and willingness to offer new opportunities to pupils who may have experienced previous difficulties. This does not mean treating all pupils the same way. Rather it takes account of pupils' varied life experiences and needs.

Our best schools seek to provide an environment where all pupils:

- learn effectively without interference or disruption
- receive respect and support at an individual level from their teachers
- gain access to all aspects of the curriculum
- know that attention is placed on their well-being
- are happy in school
- consider that their family is a part of and welcome in the school

However, none of this is achieved lightly and schools will have to recognise and overcome significant barriers to achieve a truly inclusive culture. This can only be achieved through:

- developing an understanding of how different groups perform in school

- devising clear plans and taking steps to ensure that particular groups are not disadvantaged in school and to promote their participation and success
- developing effective strategies for promoting good relationships, positive attitudes and exemplary behaviour
- addressing racism, sexism and other forms of discrimination, and what to do about cases of discrimination that do occur

In reality you know when you are in a school that truly embraces inclusion. The clues are:

- how the values of the school are reflected in its curriculum, resources, communications, procedures and conduct
- how people talk about and treat one another in the school
- the leadership provided by senior staff and the consistency of staff behaviour
- what the school intends and tries to do for 'people like me'

Creating a vision for inclusion

The following reality check will help you to create a vision for a school that will be educationally inclusive and where the teaching and learning, achievements, attitudes and well-being of every young person matter. It will steer you towards methodology that will allow you to constantly monitor and evaluate the progress each pupil makes. You should clearly identify any pupils who may be missing out, difficult to engage or feeling in some way apart from what the school seeks to provide. It will help you to consider practical steps—in the classroom and beyond—to meet pupils' needs effectively and to promote tolerance and understanding in a diverse society.

1. Are *all* pupils achieving as much as they can and deriving the maximum benefit, according to their individual needs, from what the school provides?	
2. If not, which pupils or groups of pupils are not achieving as much as they can and what are the reasons?	

3. Are the school staff aware of these issues and working to address them? If not, what needs to be done next?	

4. Can the school leadership team provide a well founded and convincing reason for the differences between groups of pupils in terms of achievement, teaching and learning, access to curricular opportunities?	

 parents

5. What action (including use of nationally funded or local initiatives) has your school taken to address these issues in order to raise the standards of pupils or groups of pupils who appear to be underachieving or at particular risk?	

6. If your school is taking action, is it appropriate and is it effective or likely to be effective? Are there any unintended consequences? How well are these consequences being handled?	

7. What action is being taken to promote racial harmony, to prepare pupils for living in a diverse and increasingly interdependent society and specifically to prevent and address racism, sexism and other forms of discrimination?	

 Now describe in broad terms what your truly inclusive school will look like in three years' time.

 Now state what will be different in one year's time.

Summary

This chapter opened with some of the recent findings from the Sutton Trust. If Britain is somewhere near the bottom of international league tables when it comes to social mobility, and the situation is not improving, then it is an appalling state of affairs. For a long time it has been accepted that the best route out of the poverty trap is education. This means that we have to ensure that every child feels included in the life of the school, that they wish to be there and see the purpose of their attendance.

Educational initiatives which are well targeted—particularly at key junctures in young people's educational careers—produce benefits worth an average £15 for every £1 spent, according to a report based on analysis by global management consulting firm, the Boston Consulting Group (*Investing for Impact: A Report on the Returns to Investments in Educational Programmes* (2007)). Their figures have been confirmed by Jones, Raby, Tolfree and Gross: 'Based on a 79% success rate, the return on investment for every pound spent on the Every Child a Reader programme is estimated to be in the region of £14.81 to £17.56' (*The Long Term Costs of Literacy Difficulties* (2006)).

These returns were measured in terms of the present value financial benefit to the individuals who take part. The analysis did not include the wider benefits to society—for example, in terms of better health, well-being and community participation—which result from these initiatives and are significant. Our best schools recognise this and in the words that introduced this chapter:

> People who say it cannot be done should not interfere with those who are doing it.

Creating a Future for Adults

Chapter 8

Creating a Vision for the Professional Learning Community

As for the best leaders, the people do not notice their existence; the next best the people honour and praise; the next the people fear; and the next the people hate. But when the best leader's work is done the people say we did it ourselves.

Lao Tse

The Prologue

Tears and Fears

A few years ago I spent a week with a local authority helping them to carry out a review of a school that was causing concern. My purpose was to watch a series of lessons and provide feedback.

The staff in the school were good people. Many of them were trying very hard to do their best for the children, to deliver national strategies and to maintain a sense of professional pride. However each and every one of them felt a sense of isolation. Uncertainty hung in the air. There was no sense of purpose or team-work. The teachers even felt uneasy in each other's company.

By the time I had seen a series of lessons that had been delivered in a most som-bre vein to pupils who seemed to lack any spark or energy, I prepared to start my walk around the school to offer feedback. The question going through my mind was, where to start? Should I tell them it was absolutely essential to smile at children if you are to create a positive learning environment? Should I tell them that children are designed to laugh a hundred times a day and that it helps them to develop a healthy body? Should I tell them that if they are happy in their work the evidence is that they will live longer? I was still pondering these points when I arrived at the door of Kate, who was a newly qualified teacher.

Very soon after our conversation had started Kate broke down in tears and she started to describe in some detail the working practices within the school.

She had not been allowed to attend training and mentoring sessions for newly qualified teachers because her place was in the classroom. She had also been told that if she needed training then she shouldn't be in a job anyway. I was clearly concerned and asked about other training opportunities within the school or from staff meetings. She said that every staff meeting consisted of the head teacher sitting behind a table and opening a security bag of mail from the Local Authority and distributing it to the collected members of staff. After this had been completed he lectured the staff about how they were responsible for declining standards in the school, poor pupil behaviour and the scruffy appearance of the building. He then regularly sent them back to their classrooms to work until 5.15 p.m. which was the time when staff meetings were scheduled to end. At that point they would be free to go home.

It quickly became clear that this poor young teacher was struggling for a variety of reasons which were largely beyond her control. As a consequence she felt totally inadequate. During the conversation she compared herself with her colleague in the other Year 4 class. This was a gentleman called Derek who was in his mid-fifties. She described him as truly fabulous, claiming that he could obtain artwork and descriptive writing of a stunning quality. She talked about detailed pen and ink sketches the children had produced of shells and how they had jotted down phrases that came into their head during the process and then incorporated them into pieces of descriptive writing that made the hairs on the back of her neck stand on end. From this point the children, who included many challenging boys, had produced the most fabulous dance work based upon the moods of the sea. As she wiped a tear from her eye she said, 'I want to be able to that. It is what the children in communities like this need, but I can only dream about it because I will never be good enough.' My heart felt heavy as I left the room, with my biggest fear being that this perceptive young teacher would simply become part of the one in four who leave the profession within three years.

My next port of call was her Year 4 colleague Derek who, according to Kate, was a very talented man. Nonetheless I found him equally despondent and feeling the same sense of inadequacy. However this time he was envious of Kate's skills. Derek was struggling to use the National Literacy framework and Qualification and Curriculum Authority (QCA) schemes of work. He found it an alien way of working. Traditionally he preferred to develop opportunities from first hand experiences and a thematic approach to the curriculum. He considered that Kate was extremely adept at developing learning within the literacy hour and he was particularly admiring of her skills on the interactive whiteboard and how the pupils in her class used ICT not as a subject but as a resource for learning. He told me that this technology was what the children of the future needed. He considered that his approaches to teaching were old hat and useless when children go home to the stimulus of 'in your face television, iPods and the internet'. He also said that the literacy subject leader had attended training at the local teaching centre but there had been no feedback. He had not been allowed to attend ICT training because the supply cover would have been too costly and because he had attended a course the previous year. Additionally he confessed that he had not taken his class into the ICT suite this school year.

Now the solution for both of these teachers was obvious. There were immediate and obvious networking, coaching and mentoring opportunities. The possibilities that could be created by these two committed teachers planning together and team teaching were phenomenal. However, I knew that this could never happen in an environment which drained the confidence out of people.

When my work for the day was completed I set off in a subdued manner into the grey evening that matched the grey day. Kate was loading her plastic box into the boot of her car. I looked across wondering if I would ever see her in schools again.

The answer was yes. Approximately four years later when I was on an interview panel for a deputy headship she breezed in as a candidate for the post. She was barely recognisable. Confidence seemed to ooze from every pore in her body. She amazed the interview panel with a visionary presentation about the future of primary education. Throughout it she showed examples of high quality work that her class had produced—work that reflected pride and perseverance, originality and creativity, independence and collaboration. The finale included a wonderful video of children performing dance based upon a huge steam engine they had seen in action during a museum visit. Throughout the process Kate moved from strength to strength and romped through the interview process to become one of the youngest deputy head teachers in the borough.

When the interview was over I saw her once again in the car park. She told me that she remembered me from visiting the school and apologised for being so emotional. However, I was more intrigued to find out what had happened to cause the transformation. She explained how the previous head had been 'eased out under a cloud' to be replaced by a dynamic new head who was absolutely committed to developing the school as a professional learning community where everyone wanted to improve, was expected to improve and had a duty to help improve others. This policy covered all the staff regardless of which position they held.

On his first day in the school he had removed the sign on his private parking space and turned it into a drop-off zone where teachers could carry heavy materials into school before parking elsewhere. After that he took a screwdriver and removed the sign on his office door saying 'Head Teacher' and took it into his first whole school assembly. He told all those within the school hall that he was replacing it with a sign saying 'Head Learner' because everyone should be a learner for all their life and they should constantly seek to improve. He then pulled out a set of bagpipes and told everyone in the assembly that he had no idea how to play them and that he certainly couldn't read music. He promised the children and the staff that he would go away and work hard and then play the bagpipes for them at the end of the year. He explained that he wanted to know what it felt like for the children as they grappled with new learning. The school had opened its doors, joined networks, affiliated with professional associations and was judged by Ofsted to be a good school with outstanding features. I was amazed to hear of the transformation and decided that I would visit the school once more to view the changes first hand.

If a school is to be outstanding it has to create a professional learning community that has an absolute passion for teaching and learning. Each adult has to strive to become better in their role whether they are a teacher, a member of the support staff, a parent or governor. It is essential that schools constantly strive to improve as a learning organisation. This chapter will help you to create this vision for the future. It describes what the best professional learning communities look like and clarifies the role of school leaders in creating them. Finally it provides a checklist which will help to shape your vision for the future.

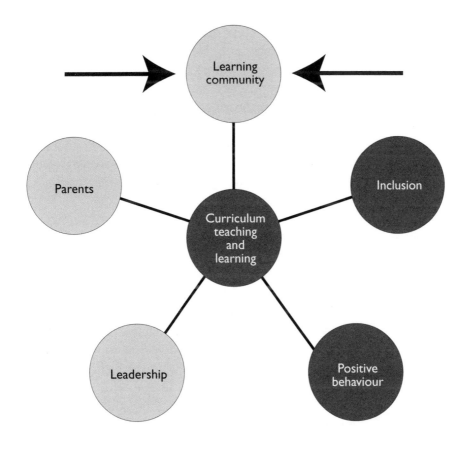

Introduction

During a recent training session, one of the delegates turned to me and said, 'I will tell you my biggest reservation about primary education today. If the framework becomes dominant in our thinking, and if the inspectors spend all their time inspecting, where will the new ideas, creativity and the magic come from in the future?'

The simple answer is that it has to come from within the organisation. The best schools ignite or reignite in their staff enthusiasm, motivation and joy in teaching and learning. They have a clear educational philosophy that is articulated and shared with the whole community. In all their work they consider the needs of the children first and the needs of adults second. In devising school improvement programmes pedagogy is considered to be at least as important as subject knowledge. Planning is developed to be a fun activity which provides teachers with energy as they seek out natural links between subjects and devise rich activities that will help children to achieve their learning objectives. The staff accept that they have a duty towards social and emotional development as well as academic achievement. When all of these qualities are in place the school will be in a wonderful position to create the right kind of education and place the individual child at the centre of all they do. Our schools need to be places where the staff are committed to creating an outstanding school. In short, everyone feels that they can improve, they have a duty to improve and a duty to improve others. When an organisation facilitates the learning of all its members through a range of high quality opportunities for all, it has the capacity to fundamentally transform education for the better.

With sadness, I argue that many schools have not taken organisational learning seriously. Research by Ofsted into continuing professional development (CPD) in schools in 2001 found that overall the main vehicle for the professional development of teachers remained course attendance. They also found that many of these opportunities consisted of loosely related activities that did not always provide good value for money or achieve the intended outcome. Schools on the whole failed to provide enough time to support effective professional development. As a consequence newly acquired knowledge and skills were not consolidated, implemented and shared with other teachers. The expected gains in pupils' knowledge, understanding and skills or specific improvements in the teachers' performance were rarely stated explicitly when the development activities were planned or used as criteria for judging their effect (Ofsted, *Continuing Professional Development for Teachers* (2001)).

There is an argument that the situation could have deteriorated further for many schools since this report was written. In the drive to raise standards much of the training provided for and within schools has been through centrally written courses relating to English and mathematics. Much of this work has been aimed at school leaders and subject leaders who have then had the task of disseminating the information within the school. This approach prevents schools from becoming autonomous organisations in terms of developing the learning community. The consequences of always working to someone else's agenda can have a demoralising effect.

> The recent climate of apportioning blame and imposing solutions has had a considerable cost. It is hard to imagine that teachers who feel deskilled, deprofessionalised and devalued can be the best promoters of children's learning.

> Kath Aspinwall, *Leading the Learning School* (1998)

I have certainly been in a few staffrooms where they may as well hang a sign above the door saying 'Abandon hope all ye who enter here'. It is argued that there are two extremes in terms of professional learning communities and these are reflected in the table below.

Outside in impoverished learning communities
• Teachers feel a sense of isolation and loneliness • There is a lack of positive feedback • The school has a sense of uncertainty • Staff avoid risk taking • There is a sense of powerlessness and the school does not feel in control of its own destiny
Inside out professional learning communities
• Collaboration, sharing, coaching and mentoring are commonplace • There is continuous formal and informal talk about pedagogy • There is a common focus • A sense of efficacy exists • There is a belief in lifelong learning • Teachers and staff value and celebrate their own learning

The simple activity below will help you to assess the state of consciousness of your own professional learning community. Consider where you are on the scale at the present time. If the clouds are grey then your only chance of making a change for the better is to stop and use this book to develop an **inside out vision** for your school. It is time to stop simply surviving; take ownership and secure your own destiny. If the skies are blue you have the absolute capacity to create an absolutely outstanding **inside out school**.

Changing the climate

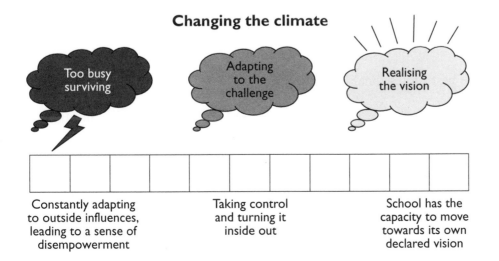

Too busy surviving	Adapting to the challenge	Realising the vision

Constantly adapting to outside influences, leading to a sense of disempowerment

Taking control and turning it inside out

School has the capacity to move towards its own declared vision

What the best professional learning communities look like

The best professional learning communities are passionate about their work and they seemingly create their own energy. On entering such a school you will feel the energy force relatively quickly. You will realise that people want to be there and the values and beliefs are shared by and modelled by everyone. There will never be significant issues relating to the recruitment and retention of staff. There will be an absolute commitment to professional development and a view that problems and difficult situations can be overcome, even those challenges that lie in the broader community. In short the following characteristics predominate:

- The staff are proud to belong and are excited and engaged in developing exciting, innovative and successful practice.
- The school has self-belief and there is clear can-do culture.
- There is collaborative leadership and a whole school commitment to developing excellent primary practice.
- Self-evaluation and self-review leads to self-challenge.
- There is a shared vision with high expectations through professional support and low tolerance of underachievement.
- Shared goals lead to shared actions and shared accountability.
- There is ongoing professional development planning for individuals, teams and the whole school.
- Appropriate resources are allocated for the professional development of all staff.
- There is formal and informal peer coaching and shared learning leading to informed professional dialogue about pedagogy.
- Clear communication and dissemination processes exist.
- Each and every member of staff has good practice that is worthy of dissemination to others.

The best professional learning communities achieve this through:

- Making the best use of nationally produced materials ensuring that use is personalised to the needs of the school.
- Appropriately using Local Authority personnel, advice training and data.
- Pertinent research and external consultancy.
- Devising and joining networks of schools and making use of leading teachers.

- Developing and promoting a staff library of published and web based resources.
- The appropriate allocation of funding.
- Ensuring that all staff are included and feel part of the whole school team.

Too regularly we work in an environment where we are seeking the next quick-fix in order to impact on the next set of results. We look for quick programmes to enable a borderline child to move from a level 3 to a level 4 in the national tests. The process is more complex than that and **inside out schools** recognise this.

Becoming and remaining a good teacher is demanding. We are in a rapidly changing world where new programmes of study are evolving. Our knowledge of how the human brain develops is growing. We need to make increasingly good use of the new technologies available to us. As a consequence it is absolutely essential that the school makes a commitment to individual, team and staff learning. It is also important to develop an open, supportive and collaborative culture across the school that raises self-esteem, confidence and enthusiasm. Research has frequently shown that:

- Where teaching is already of a higher quality there is often a desire amongst staff to continue their own learning, increasing the capacity for self and school improvement.
- The school that promotes itself as a professional learning community will recruit the best staff. It will also retain many of them whilst more ambitious teachers will move on to become school leaders in their own right. This will increase the system's capacity to produce further outstanding schools.
- Children are far more likely to develop a desire and enthusiasm for life-long learning when they see teachers modelling it on a regular basis.

The role of school leaders

Where leadership and management are weak or ineffective within a school it is much harder to do a good job as a teacher. Therefore the challenge for **inside out schools** is to ensure that they are always making the job of teaching easier. Where leadership is effective both teachers and pupils will be better motivated, people know what is going on because communication is clear and frequent and everyone feels they are pulling together and working towards shared goals. **Inside out school leaders** recognise this and use three significant strategies to support this aspect of their work:

Modelling

The best school leaders recognise that it is absolutely essential to use the power of example. School leaders who model desired practice will influence staff and pupils alike. Teachers watch what their leaders do very closely. Far more critical forces than Ofsted inspectors sit in school staffrooms every breaktime. Teachers are always checking the consistency of their leader's actions to check that what they say. Teachers want their leaders to be successful and they want leaders who can 'walk the talk'. In order to set a good example school leaders must be able to do what they ask others to do. This will involve teaching some lessons, delivering powerful assemblies and being high profile around the school often from early morning to late evening.

Not only are leaders closely observed by teachers but the staff also carefully observe what they pay attention to. Head teachers and other school leaders who do not visit classrooms on a regular basis are quickly judged by their colleagues to be uninterested in teaching and learning. By contrast it is possible for school leaders to demonstrate that their prime focus is teaching and learning through regular classroom visits and conversations with pupils and teachers. As a primary head teacher between 1987 and 1999 it was my aim to visit every classroom every day. Colleagues now tell me that this is no longer possible. However, I did recently visit a very successful primary school with high contextual value added scores where the head teacher proudly proclaimed that he spent a significant amount of time each day 'strolling about' in classrooms. In reality he was carrying out highly effective learning walks.

Monitoring

The school that knows and understands itself is capable of solving its own problems. School leaders use a variety of strategies to carry out this work including the analysis of data and school trends, work scrutiny, pupil and parent surveys, and the direct observation of teaching and learning and providing feedback. Whilst this needs to be judgemental and is often a key part of performance management structures, the real challenge is to make it a developmental activity for teachers. Inspections have regularly demonstrated that where monitoring is effective the overall quality of teaching is higher.

Where monitoring is non-existent or poor and infrequent the quality of teaching and learning is lower. The observation of lessons and other self-evaluation strategies allow school leaders to develop a substantial knowledge of the individual teacher's strengths and development needs. The best leaders work hard to ensure that these development needs are met and the appropriate support is brokered. This is often at its best when provided in-house through peer coaching, mentoring and professional support because the school considers that it is autonomous and self-improving. This provides the organisation with internal energy and a clear sense of optimism.

Dialogue

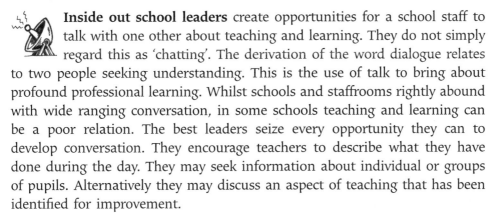 **Inside out school leaders** create opportunities for a school staff to talk with one other about teaching and learning. They do not simply regard this as 'chatting'. The derivation of the word dialogue relates to two people seeking understanding. This is the use of talk to bring about profound professional learning. Whilst schools and staffrooms rightly abound with wide ranging conversation, in some schools teaching and learning can be a poor relation. The best leaders seize every opportunity they can to develop conversation. They encourage teachers to describe what they have done during the day. They may seek information about individual or groups of pupils. Alternatively they may discuss an aspect of teaching that has been identified for improvement.

Describing to a colleague the work we have carried out can be very demanding. However, research has shown that it is insightful to both the listener and speaker. In retelling events we often learn things that we had not previously been aware of. It is the process of telling it out loud that raises issues within our mind. Too often our best teachers have found it extremely difficult to have the self-knowledge to articulate what makes their classrooms special places. This is often because there have been insufficient opportunities to do this. Dialogue brings opportunities to discover this self-knowledge and therefore the capacity to articulate what constitutes high quality practice. It provides the opportunities to bring to the fore our thinking, philosophies, understanding and assumptions. Dialogue makes our inner skills and knowledge explicit. This is important because while it remains implicit we can neither share it nor use it as a resource for ourselves or others.

It is absolutely essential that the dialogue is a two-way process and not seen as a form of interrogation. The process should be used to provide encouragement and feedback as well as questioning about teaching. It is also essential to provide direct guidance to colleagues. School leaders should never fight shy of investing their own intellectual capital in developing teachers, especially those in the early stages of their career. Classrooms are busy, exciting and dynamic places where much happens in short periods of time. There are often insufficient opportunities to make sense of it all and thus develop professional craft. Dialogue helps us to process daily actions and to learn from them.

 ## Developing a vision for the professional learning community

Here are two questions for you:

1. In a ten-teacher primary school where each teacher has worked for ten years, how does any single teacher tap into the other ninety years of experience?
2. How do you create a school where everyone thinks they can improve, has a duty to improve and a duty to improve others?

The answer lies in devising a vision that plans for the future development of the professional learning community over the next three years. Our most effective schools, regardless of phase or size, have a vision that shapes the future of their professional learning communities. They have a clear picture of what they are trying to create and then take actions to bring the dream to reality through developing the appropriate systems and processes. In this way they create the learning culture of the school.

For the process to be effective we need a culture of collaboration where everyone is responsible for the creation of the vision, and then bringing it to life. The table below will help the process to commence. It should start with an analysis of the current situation. This should include the positives and the negatives—it is important to celebrate the present successes because these are easier to build upon.

The activity will help you to shape a vision for the future development of your professional learning community. Ideally it should be carried out by the full school community including the governing body. The prompts may be helpful; however they are certainly not exclusive. The exercise places a clear emphasis on developing strategies which promote staff well-being and self-esteem. These are absolutely essential. There is a clear relationship between staff well-being and pupil achievement.

What are your current strengths? Which of these areas need to improve over the next three years?

Do staff ...
- have high self-esteem and confidence and feel valued and supported in their work?
- experience a wide range of CPD opportunities within the organisation and through other organisations and networks?
- talk about and celebrate staff learning?
- value their own learning, expect to learn and actively seek it?
- learn from each other?
- see the leadership team as learners making changes for the better?

Does school leadership ...
- ensure that the organisation's learning leads to embedded change?
- have regular periods of reflection which shapes new learning?
- improve the learning of the wider community (e.g. parents, governors)?
- model a commitment to the learning of all?
- provide monitoring programmes which offer high quality feedback and future development opportunities?
- use dialogue to promote a passion for teaching and learning?

In three years' time what sensations will your staff feel in order to be effective and inspirational?

Possible responses include:
- Confident
- Positive
- Empowered
- Valued
- Inspired
- Inspirational

- Trusted
- Proud
- Energised
- Skilled
- Cared for

What strategies, opportunities and experiences need to be in place in three years' time to achieve this?

Possible responses include:
- Clearly articulated and disseminated vision
- Clearly identified CPD programme for each member of staff
- Emphasis placed on high quality relationships
- Teamwork on planning and seeking solutions to problems
- Action on staff well-being and working environment, support to manage stress
- Leadership responds appropriately to staff and pupil views
- Staff have full understanding of the hidden curriculum and recognise the implications of indirect action
- Coaching/mentoring opportunities
- Supportive positive management strategies including teams and groups with regular positive feedback
- Regular access to external expertise
- Access to sustained and focused CPD opportunities that embed practice in line with school policy
- Leadership opportunities for all with the right collaboration for the right purpose
- Networking opportunities

 Now in broad terms describe your vision for the professional learning community in three years' time.

 Now state what will be different in one year's time, ensuring that these are identified in the school improvement plan.

Summary

Our best teachers are people who are strongly committed to their own learning and development. They will bring reflection and evaluation into their practice. They require and thrive on the company of fellow learners. They will look for both challenge and support from others and seek to create new skills, knowledge and understanding together. Their commitment and energy will be greatly enhanced when they are a part of team and utilise organisational learning. In short, our best teachers will be found in or will have flourished in high quality professional learning communities. This is because they create the right climate for success. There are other teachers who have the capacity to become excellent but who have lost their energy and sense of direction because of the environment in which they work.

The only way to create an outstanding school is to invest in individual and organisational learning. **Inside out leaders** fully recognise their role in the process. They recognise the need to empower and build expertise and confidence in others rather than seek self-glory thus enabling the following to become true:

> As for the best leaders, the people do not notice their existence; the next best the people honour and praise; the next the people fear; and the next the people hate. But when the best leader's work is done the people say we did it ourselves.
>
> Lao Tse

Creating a Vision for the Professional Learning Community

Chapter 9
Creating a Vision for Leadership

Leadership is action not position.

Fred Trueman

The Prologue

The Prime Minister's Delivery Unit

It was 7.30 a.m. and I was awaiting the arrival of a train from King's Cross carrying two senior officials from the Primary National Strategy and two members of the Prime Minister's Delivery Unit. They were visiting our Local Authority to assess the impact of the work we had carried out to date in implementing the government's programmes.

As the train arrived I quickly recognised the party and moved towards them. I introduced myself to the people I had not previously met, and then we exchanged pleasantries. I welcomed them to Yorkshire; we spoke of the weather and the joys of GNER trains. However the discussions quickly moved on and I became aware that absolutely everything I said was being written down by a smart young man called Christian from the Delivery Unit. Before we had left the station platform I had been asked whether the authority would experience an increase in the number of schools achieving the national floor targets in the summer. Whilst we were in the station concourse I was asked if the new target setting arrangements were producing extra rigour and challenge. As we climbed into the car for the next part of the journey I was asked if the council had a policy of closing under performing schools.

As we drove the ten miles into the Local Authority the questions came thick and fast and pages of notes were taken. During the day we were scheduled to visit schools, meet with a group of head teachers and hold interviews with other education officers. As we neared one school we reached the top of a hill and started the sharp descent which took us past a huge steel works, an Asda superstore and a clothing supplier known locally as 'the knickers factory', whereupon Christian stopped grilling me on issues relating to educational standards and asked if we were in the Yorkshire Dales. Clearly he was expecting James Herriott or Gervase Phinn to come around the corner. Dave—a genial man from the Primary National Strategy, with a clear understanding of the needs of children—physically bit on his sleeve and tried not to laugh. I politely explained the Dales were about sixty miles to the north.

We toured the first school and it was a fabulous experience. I listened to a group of Year 4 telling me how they were carrying out a study of the river and canal which flowed past their school. I was particularly interested by the fact that they had recently visited a derelict factory, drawn sketches and then used the experience to devise story settings. They read their work to me and the hairs on the back of my neck seemed to tingle with the quality of their work.

As we returned to the head teacher's office Christian's questions started once more. The school had recently joined a Primary Learning Network and he asked what the impact would be on this year's results. Then he asked if there was enough rigour in Fischer Family Trust D predictions to allow the school to set sufficiently challenging targets. Finally he asked the question that proved to be the straw that broke the camel's back: 'At what stage will you be abandoning the wider curriculum to provide booster classes, revision books and extra homework so that the children achieve well in the statutory and optional tests?'

The head teacher drew herself up to her full five feet four inches and stated very clearly that the children in her school received just one childhood and that she was absolutely determined that it was going to be a magical one. She pointed out that there were significant problems within the locality and that it was the school's duty to promote curiosity and a sense of awe, wonder and spirituality, because nobody else could be relied on to do it. She stated categorically that the school would not be abandoning the wider curriculum at any stage to provide extra time for revision and booster work. The she pointed out that part of her rationale for this came from the government's own publications. *Excellence and Enjoyment* had declared that government and local authorities needed to take pressure off schools, take a sensible approach to testing and target setting and take ownership of the curriculum to ensure all pupils receive rich and vivid learning experiences. Christian did not write those comments down.

The school achieved very good results in the tests that summer and in the following autumn they received a glowing report from Ofsted.

The striking feature about this head teacher is that she knew exactly what the children and the community needed. She knew exactly what she was trying to create. She had the capacity to lead the school to a better future through directing, influencing and inspiring the work of others. This allowed her to distribute leadership throughout the school whilst ensuring that everybody was empowered and accountable for delivering the school's declared aims, policies and practices, thus increasing the capacity for future leadership.

This chapter takes you though processes that will help you to achieve the same.

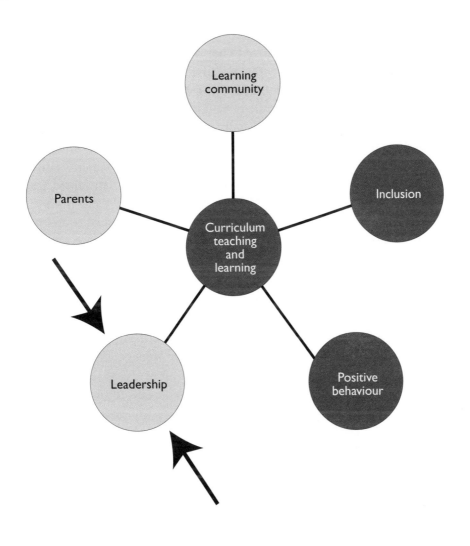

Introduction

In his autobiography, *As It Was*, Fred Trueman claimed that 'leadership is action not position'. OK, so the former Yorkshire and England fast bowler may not be the greatest expert on primary education but the quote is significant. Too many people see leadership as a position they hold within an organisation, whereas it should be a verb rather than a noun. Leadership should be lively, vibrant, purposeful and above all else should be taking you to a new and better future. The amount of research and writing about leadership has been phenomenal over recent years. The government has established the multi-million pound National College for School Leadership. So here is a controversial thought to start the chapter: I believe that the vast majority of primary schools have been *managed* rather than *led* over the last twenty years. Since the Education Reform Act of 1988 schools have simply managed wave after wave of government initiative. They have managed the implementation of several rewrites of the National Curriculum. They have managed the implementation of the National Literacy and Mathematics Strategies and the subsequent Primary National Strategy. They have coped with new financial arrangements, various Ofsted frameworks and formats for inspection. They have adapted and adopted new powers for local authorities and now the Every Child Matters agenda. Schools have been forced to manage rather than lead because of the pace of legislation. In addition, too many head teachers are fearful of trying to create something different to the perceived norm. The government itself hinted at the problems when it published *Excellence and Enjoyment* in 2004, which stated:

> Teachers already have great freedoms to exercise their professional judgement about how they teach. Many teachers believe that Ofsted or the QCA effectively restrict that freedom.
>
> Department for Education and Skills (DfES), *Excellence and Enjoyment: A Strategy for Primary Schools* (2003)

The Ofsted framework for inspecting schools published in 2005 and its current Self-Evaluation Form has once again linked leadership and management together when in reality they are very different. The current criteria used to judge a school's effectiveness is clearly based more on management rather than leadership. There is a focus on self-evaluation, the smooth running of the school, the allocation of resources and vetting procedures. Whist all of this is important, the emphasis is on looking backwards over your shoulder rather than steering the school towards an outstanding future. By contrast, previous frameworks devoted a whole section to school leadership. For example, to secure a judgement of very good leadership within the 2003 framework you had demonstrate that you were innovative, could articulate a clear vision for the school in the future resulting in strategic thinking and planning for improvement.

Therefore the first challenge is to be clear about what we mean by the term leadership. This on its own can be an elusive challenge. Here come my first three quotations on this issue. As early as 1974 Stodgill stated: 'There are almost as many definitions of leadership as there are persons who have attempted to define the concept.'

The number of definitions has clearly grown since that point. The internet abounds with them and this text makes reference to just a handful of them. Bennis and Nanus (1997) confirmed this confused situation further by stating: 'Leadership is like the abominable snowman whose footprints are everywhere but who is nowhere to be seen.' In an analysis of ninety successful people in public life they found that:

> There appeared to be no obvious pattern for their success. They were right brained, left brained, tall and short, fat and thin, articulate and inarticulate, assertive and retiring, dressed for success and dressed for failure, participative and autocratic. There were more variations than themes. Even their managerial styles were restlessly different.
>
> W. Bennis and B. Nanus,
> *Leaders: Strategies for Taking Charge* (1997)

Leadership in inside out schools is about a journey to achieve a vision

Leadership is about a journey. It is about taking people to a defined better future. That is why vision and leadership are closely linked. Head teachers often have compelling personal visions. However, too few schools actually have clear statements of vision which are lucid and articulated and disseminated to others. When the former Teacher Training Authority identified the skills and attributes of headship the first statement related to vision. They stated that head teachers should be able to create and secure a clear and effective vision for the institution. School leaders need to be able to create a vision for the school that helps it to meet its fundamental purpose and aid the development of the community it serves. So here are my next three quotations that support this view:

> A leader shapes and shares a vision which gives point to the work of others.
>
> Charles Handy

> Leadership is the capacity to translate vision into reality.
>
> Warren G. Bennis

> Leaders are individuals who establish direction for a working group of individuals, who gain commitment from these groups of members to this direction and who then motivate these members to achieve the direction's outcomes.
>
> J. A. Conger

Leadership in inside out schools is about engaging others in a journey in order to achieve vision

The last of the definitions above introduces the notion of directing the work of others. The traditional model of primary school leadership had the head teacher at the top of the organisation who represented authority. In reality they were often deemed to be the sole leader. They directed the work of those beneath them. Many actively sheltered their staff from the outside world, dealing with wide ranging issues including angry parents or the demands being made by the Local Authority. In many ways they seemed to hold a maternal/paternal role with pupils and adults alike. The Ministry of Education in 1959 exemplified this parenting role when it wrote:

> In the training of teachers the Head often finds himself in a position not unlike that of a practiced craftsman with his apprentices. It is his responsibility to launch young teachers on their careers, and their confidence in their own powers and happiness in their profession may be largely determined by his example, sympathy and tactful help.
>
> *Primary Education*, 1959

However, times have changed. Expectations for primary schools, and those who work in them, have never been higher. They will continue to rise further. This is the era where external monitoring predominates, where parents will move their children if they are unhappy with the education provided, solicitors will leaflet parents at the school gate to see if they wish to take legal action against the school and television cameras will poke their lenses through school railings at the hint of a bad news story. Strangely much of this causes me no problems, although it is always a shame that the millions of good news stories about schools fail to get the same attention. Schools are now in greater competition for pupils. They advertise their wares through websites and produce their own news bulletins. School leaders are responsible for setting and operating their own budget. As a consequence schools need leadership systems that are every bit as good as those in industry if they are to firstly survive and secondly thrive. They need to be constantly improving in order to offer a better service to children, parents and communities. This can only be achieved through ensuring that there is a model of empowered, accountable, distributive leadership. The head teacher of the twenty-first century recognises that the more power he or she gives away to others the more power he/she will have for school improvement.

In a typical primary school there is a need for many leaders. Traditionally there will be a head teacher, deputy or assistant head teacher, other members of the senior leadership team, subject leaders and a special educational needs coordinator. However, depending upon the size of the school, its needs and access to additional funding, there could be many different leaders. In a relatively small one-form entry primary school there could easily be up to thirty identified leaders. This is reflected in the list below:

Possible leadership positions in primary schools

- Head teacher
- Deputy head teacher
- Assistant head teacher
- Chair of governors
- Clerk to governors
- School council
- A leader for each key stage
- Special educational needs coordinator
- Assessment coordinator
- Extended schools coordinator
- Leader of support staff including teaching assistants and learning mentors
- Bursar

- A leader for each National Curriculum subject area plus Religious Education
- Continuing professional development leader
- Year group leaders
- Enterprise education champion
- Performance management leaders
- Behaviour improvement leader
- Lead teacher for Gifted and Talented pupils
- Leading teacher for intervention
- Lead person for administrative staff
- Senior school meals supervisor
- Site manager

The first challenge is to ensure that there is a dynamic and vibrant senior leadership team that is fully fit for purpose. The membership of this team sometimes needs to be flexible so that it provides the right collaboration for the right purpose. People in the leadership team of **inside out schools** are not there for historical reasons or because they are amongst the highest paid. The senior leadership team should consist of those dynamic individuals who will secure the school's future. It could include teaching assistants or learning mentors or those in the early stages of their career who have clear potential to lead schools in the future.

Each member of the leadership team should have clear set of responsibilities. The traditional model is often based on the key stages. This means that the team could consist of head teacher, deputy, early years foundation stage leader, Key Stage 1 leader and Key Stage 2 leader. Alternatively those schools that have been part of the National Strategy's Primary Leadership Programme may well have a leadership team of head teacher, deputy head, literacy subject leader and mathematics subject leader. A model that I encountered recently had each member of the leadership team responsible for developing one of the school aims. There was a clear rationale for this. School aims are often carefully devised but quickly forgotten. It was seen as a strategy for keeping the aims high profile. All three models have their merits because people become accountable for ensuring good practice and the development of a particular aspect of the school. However, I would like to propose a different model which stresses leadership as an action that leads you to a better future.

The inside out school's model for developing a school leadership team with distributed and accountable leadership

The model below will help you to drive school improvement forward. It develops the notion that leadership is active and therefore is better considered as a verb rather than a noun.

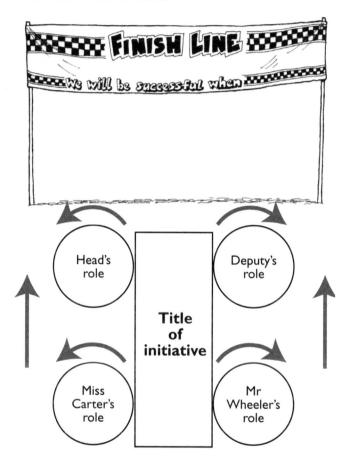

The model is based on the concept of a vehicle with flattened wheels—when each wheel is turning in the direction of the arrow it will propel the vehicle towards the defined finishing line. Each person on the leadership team has a clearly defined role and their tasks are written within their wheel. However, the names are interchangeable according to the task being carried out or the initiative being led. The personnel are also changeable. This leadership team creates the right collaboration for the right purpose. Extra wheels can be added. Alternatively, an extra person can pull the vehicle from the front or push from behind. If any person fails to carry out their work in a suitable manner it acts as a brake to the process or potentially sends the vehicle in the wrong direction. This approach clearly identifies the responsibilities of each person and emphasises their responsibilities to each other. Following the stages below will help you to carry out this process.

1. Identify the key initiatives the school leadership team will be working on over the coming months. This should be limited to three or four highly significant actions.
2. When this has been done the leadership team needs to have a blank copy of the above diagram for each initiative. The title of the initiative is placed in the centre.
3. The school devises clear success criteria for the initiative being addressed. This should be expressed in clear, unambiguous statements that build from the stem: *We will be successful when...* This will represent the finishing line for the vehicle.
4. Write down the key actions that each person will be carrying out when within their wheel. Add further wheels if necessary or have a person pulling from the front or pushing from behind.
5. Review the progress being made on a regular basis.

I recently used this model with a school which was approximately six months away from an Ofsted inspection. The school had been part of a recent amalgamation and therefore had a relatively new leadership team and roles and responsibilities were underdeveloped. The school was also in a vulnerable position because results were lower than other similar schools. Ofsted praised the approaches taken to driving improvement stating they had brought considerable clarity to the work of the school's leaders. They also reported that school leaders had a secure understanding of the school's strengths and weaknesses and had intervened vigorously to improve progress. The refocusing of the school improvement plan on a small number of success measures was beneficial.

The model described can ensure that all senior leaders are galvanised into appropriate action. However, there remains the significant challenge of distributing power to others within the school. In 2004, Geoff Southworth of the National College for School Leadership wrote:

We need lots of leaders in schools and we already have them. The problem is that too often leadership is confined to head, deputy and subject leaders. Too often leadership is seen as being only for those in particular positions in the schools. Without doubt these colleagues are and should be leaders, but this sometimes blinds us to the fact that other colleagues also perform leadership roles. The difference is that they are informal leaders and they exercise their leadership from time to time. The idea of distributed leadership is that we need lots of leaders in schools.

Learning Centred Leadership (2004)

Each school will need a raft of school leaders beyond the leadership team, many of which will have been listed above. **Inside out schools** ensure that each one is appropriately line managed with meeting times set and full performance management systems in place. They ensure that all those people in leadership roles:

- Consider the development of pedagogy that brings about learning as their priority
- Understand the vision and engage in strategic thinking
- Collaborate effectively with other colleagues
- Monitor and evaluate systematically
- Reflect on and are affected by school culture
- Are agents of change
- Make a difference to learning at a whole school level
- Plan to constantly improve all the above areas

The diagram demonstrating driving school improvement is easily transferable from the leadership team to other initiatives within the school and focuses the best people to work on appropriate tasks. Whilst a small primary school could have thirty different leadership posts, in reality there may not be thirty members of staff. This is where creative approaches to grouping responsibilities can become necessary and also provide a school with strength. For example, many schools maintain the traditional model for subject leadership. However, school inspectors still regularly find subject leadership to be of concern during assessments. As a consequence, innovative schools are increasingly those schools which are grouping subjects and aspects of the curriculum.

In a school I visited recently they had one subject leader for each of the core subjects and ICT. In addition they had one person leading the arts and physical education and another member of staff covering the humanities (including geography, history and religious education). A fourth member of staff promoted work on the social and emotional aspects of learning, citizenship and enterprise education.

Another school that was keen to ensure that subject leaders are more empowered set up weeks where evidence trails took place. During the week a subject leader would work with a member of the governing body to collect evidence from within their subject. This would incorporate the observation of teaching, work scrutiny, analysis of planning, pupil interviews and leading a work assembly within the subject. At the end of the process a report was given to the leadership team outlining strengths, areas for development and a clear timescale for future developments. The governor involved on the process reported back to the full governing body. The school covered three areas each term. Recently this has been extended to include the social and emotional aspects of learning and behaviour.

When leadership is genuinely distributed within a school it becomes a much more efficient organisation. The most frequent challenge in moving towards a model of genuine distributed leadership is that people at the top of the organisation are reluctant to let go. This can be understandable because the overall accountability will always come back to them. The alternative though is unacceptable. If school leaders try to do everything themselves they will become overloaded and struggle to cope. The pressure will become unbearable. However, there is a much more powerful reason to let go. Chapter 8 stressed the absolute importance of developing the school as a professional learning community. A model of distributed leadership enhances this process. Letting go does not mean abdicating responsibility. As school leaders encourage and promote distributed leadership in others they will be devoting time and energy to coaching and developing leadership skills across the whole workforce. A further consequence will be that there will be occasions where other members of staff will have greater knowledge skills and expertise than the head or members of the leadership team. This can be a difficult pill to swallow for those who have control freak tendencies, but it is an extremely healthy sign for a professional learning community.

So having discussed the concept of distributed leadership, here are my next three quotations to support it as a model for the future development of primary schools.

> Leadership is a process of influence between a leader and those who are followers.
>
> Edwin Hollander, *Leadership Dynamics* (1978)

> Leadership is an attempt at influencing the activities of followers through the communication process and toward the attainment of some goal or goals.
>
> J. H. Donelly, J. M. Ivancevich and J. L. Gibson, *Organizations: Behavior, Structure, Processes* (1985)

> Leadership is not a person or a position. It is a complex moral relationship between people, based on trust, obligation, commitment, emotion, and a shared vision of the good.
>
> Joanne B. Ciulla, *The Heart of Leadership* (1998)

Each of these quotes introduces another key aspect of leadership which relates to how leaders influence and inspire the work of others.

 ## Leadership in inside out schools is about influencing and inspiring others so that they are engaged in a journey in order to achieve vision

Of course there are many different ways of distributing leadership. It can actually be done in a direct autocratic style. Roles and responsibilities are given out and made clear and there is no need for discussion. Expectations are therefore set and there will be consequences for not carrying out the job in the expected manner. However, this model does not necessarily bode well for a happy working environment and it can help lead to recruitment issues because the reputation of the school's leadership stops people applying for posts in the school. Sometimes retention is not an issue because staff are too frightened to tell their head that they are looking to move on. I have heard this form of autocratic leadership referred to as the 'sunshine model', as in: 'I have told you what to do, now go away and do it, Sunshine!'

This strategy was probably employed by the late football manager Brian Clough who once said: 'When I have a disagreement with someone we sit down and discuss it man to man, and then decide that I was right.'

This however is not the approach for distributed leadership in **inside out schools**. Here the approach is about inspirational leadership that wins hearts and minds. As stated previously it is the professional learning community that makes the significant difference to a school. Therefore it is the people who matter. The distribution of leadership and power has the capacity to build relationships, whereas an uneven power base simply distorts relationships. I accept that head teachers have to make a range of decisions some of which will be necessarily unilateral. Sometimes these can be lonely decisions to take. It is always the case that the good leader will come out on top at times of significant conflict. However, other decisions they will quite rightly abdicate to others. Research into leadership shows that new and less experienced head teachers are more likely to make unilateral decisions than collaborative ones, whilst more successful head teachers give more decision making powers away as they become more expert. Terry Mahony sums up the real challenge for school leaders when he asks the following questions:

- Don't you think you should monitor the physical and psychological health of the school you lead?
- With the growth of target setting in teaching and learning, could you develop and publish performance indicators for these to dimensions of the school?
- Would measures such as incidence of smiling, rates of illness and absence, laughing levels have a place in your school improvement plan?
- Do you lead ethically?
- Do your decisions engage the self-respect of your colleagues or diminish it?
- Does your behaviour develop personal integrity in your relationships and professional courage in your staff?
- Does what you do open up or close down the capabilities of others?

Terry Mahony, *Principled Leadership* (2004)

So what are the key skills that the leader needs in order to create a vision for the future which is articulated to all and energises people to move forward?

The first is to have a personal vision of how primary education will be different in the future. The second is to have a rich array of strategies and personal qualities which will allow you to succeed. The aim is not to impose vision but to negotiate vision. In the early days of a new headship, a newly appointed leader could find themselves working in a school with several visions as people pull in different directions. If leadership is weak this will continue into the future. Each member of staff could have a personal vision and approach that they find perfectly valid. The task becomes to discover and manage this diversity so that a single vision can emerge. The activities within this book have been tried and tested and should lead to high quality dialogue that will shape future direction. However, we must not diminish the true size of the challenge.

Roy Leighton writing in *Primary Practice* (2004) referred to the 10-40-40-10 rule. This refers to how average percentages of people will respond to change. He cleverly links his argument to the characters in *Winnie the Pooh*.

- The first ten per cent are the Tiggers. In my mind these people simply bound around the place full of glee. These are the risk takers who are up for any challenge and have very little fear of failure. These people can be the powerhouse for the school because they provide passion which they turn into energy.

- The next forty per cent of staff are very much in favour of change and development, but only with the right structure, support and training. These are the Kangas. They will ask questions to achieve clarity because they will not automatically accept another initiative (especially if they see Tiggers bouncing around the place brimming with enthusiasm). Every school needs Kangas because they bring logic, systems and processes to an initiative. They bring the commitment that will take the project to completion and full fruition. They are potentially invaluable to the school and that is why school leaders must harness their full support.

- The next forty per cent are the Eeyores. These are the people who aren't malicious in any form and are perfectly safe. They are however often uncomfortable with change. They do not take risks readily and are insecure about situations they are not used to. They reluctantly join in with initiatives; however, they are certainly not going to be the people pulling from the front. Overall they are popular enough in the staffroom but are a critical group to work with if change is to be achieved.

• The final ten per cent are made up of Owls (or 'Wols' to give them their true title). They appear to have an air of perceived wisdom, even though they may not be the most intellectual of people. Each Owl may come with a different set of beliefs and values. However, they are going to be hard work and stubborn about change because generally they believe there is only one way to proceed, and that is their way. They will challenge decisions both openly and through indirect ways which can make them dangerously influential.

The reality is that you are required to influence a wide range of people and therefore a wide range of skills and strategies are required. However, I have found the list below helpful in securing support for innovation.

School leaders make a difference when:

• Their focus on teaching and learning is persistent and consistent.

• Leadership is clearly differentiated according to the context of the school based upon its community and location, the range of key stages, the immediate history of the school, religious affiliations and so on.

• They are optimistic, positive and passionate. It has often been said that the best leaders have unwarranted optimism.

• Their work is person-centred and, if you believe in the way Roy Leighton classifies teachers above, you work with everyone on a whole school, team and individual basis. It has been said that a school staff is made up of radiators (who give out warmth and energy) and drains (who drain the spirit out of others); the answer with the latter group is to work with them and not to shy away from one-to-one dialogue. The challenge remains to engage hearts and minds.

• People do leadership rather than headship because leadership is a function and not a role. The challenge is to constantly seek out and develop the other leaders, especially those who are opinion formers or those who come to the fore when a crisis occurs.

• They clearly demonstrate a sense of direction and purpose ensuring constant movement and improvement. In these schools leadership is a verb rather than a noun.

- There is a relentless focus on children's achievements and progress within a broad range of contexts because this is what differentiates the school from any other organisation.

So leadership is about taking people and an organisation to a better future. It is achieved in part through the way in which you direct people but it is most effective when the leader influences the hearts and minds of others. Getting the balance right in how you direct and work with others and how you proceed with the task at hand is absolutely essential. This is reflected in the diagram below which is based on the work of Roger Blake and Jane Mouton.

In *The New Managerial Grid* (1978), Blake and Mouton devised five simple possible outcomes of leadership:

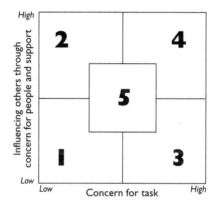

The outcomes are marked by the numbers on the grid:

1. *Impoverished leadership* where everyone does the minimum to get by.
2. *Country club leadership* where so much attention is paid to satisfying relationships that the task may be neglected.
3. *Authority and obedience* where the emphasis is on completing the task and ignoring the needs of the people.
4. *Team leadership* where committed staff work together for common purposes.
5. *Organisational and person leadership* where completing the task and maintaining relationships and influencing others work hand in hand. This is the approach of the **inside out school leader**.

So are you ready for the final three quotes about leadership that confirm this view?

> A leader takes people where they want to go. A great leader takes people where they don't necessarily want to go, but ought to be.
>
> Rosalynn Carter, US First Lady (1977–81)

> Leadership (according to John Sculley) revolves around vision, ideas, direction, and has more to do with inspiring people as to direction and goals than with day-to-day implementation. A leader must be able to leverage more than his own capabilities. He must be capable of inspiring other people to do things without actually sitting on top of them with a checklist.
>
> W. Bennis, *On Becoming a Leader* (1989)

> Leadership is a process whereby an individual influences a group of individuals to achieve a common goal.
>
> P. G. Northouse, *Leadership Theory and Practice* (2004)

Leadership in inside out schools develops vision to improve capacity

Every year leadership teams in primary schools write their annual school improvement plan. Within it many of them will consider strategies to raise attainment and standards, improve the quality of teaching and learning, and develop key aspects of the national strategy and frameworks. Some schools will draw up plans to improve subject leadership but only the best schools actually carry out a full analysis of the current strengths and weaknesses within school leadership and draw up plans to improve leadership, thus creating a vision of school leadership for the future. Once the vision is drawn up for leadership and strategies are devised to achieve it, the school monitors and evaluates its progress.

Inside out school leaders seek to influence and inspire all those who work there because in the context of the primary school the ends do not justify the means. The checklist below will allow you to carry out a reality check on your current situation and develop a vision for school leadership in the future.

	Comments relating to the current reality	What will be different in three years' time?
School leaders have high but not complacent self-esteem, optimism and believe they can	Not high enough	
Leadership is driven by a sense of moral purpose and principle that aids the development of vision	Need to make this more apparent to the others	
Leaders have a clear understanding of the distinctive nature of the school community and its needs	need to be more reflective	
The school has a clear written vision statement based upon these needs	✓	
The vision is articulated and disseminated to all (including pupils, parents, governors)	✓	
The vision has created common aspirations that are understood by all	✓	
These aspirations are turned into reality in all areas and aspects of the school's work	✓	
All staff have sufficiently high expectations	✓	
The leadership team (and others) have low tolerance of underachievement (staff and pupils)	need to be more intolerant and not shy away from difficult discussions	
Leadership is sufficiently focused on teaching and learning	✓	
The quality of teaching is constantly improving (in all areas) and is good or better in seventy-five per cent of classrooms	✓ - need to develop my own	
When necessary leadership challenges orthodoxy to achieve the right results for the community	BBB - need to develop further	

	Comments relating to the current reality	What will be different in three years' time?
Leadership generates positive relations with all (including parents and wider community), so that all have optimism and confidence	Y3,4 ✓	
Inspiration, dialogue and team working transforms practice	develop	transform
Leadership creates effective collaborations within school and learns through other networks	✓	
There is distributed, empowered and accountable leadership with clear line management structures	✓	
This leads to the full school community being engaged	/	
School leadership inspires others thus engaging their hearts and minds	Y3,4 ✓	Y5,6
As a consequence teachers recognise and welcome opportunities to be creative and innovative in the way they teach and shape young lives	developing	
This leads to pupils that are well-motivated, enjoy learning and achieve well		
All school leaders monitor and evaluate their work in order to improve		

 Now describe in broad terms what leadership will be like in your school in three years' time.

 Now state what will be different in one year's time, making sure you incorporate these developments into your school improvement plan.

Summary

The challenge in creating a vision for leadership is not to confuse it with management—the day-to-day running of the school, the deployment of staff and school and self-evaluation are all essential management characteristics. Leadership creates a vision for a better future and then directs and influences others to achieve the vision. The model of leadership used in **inside out schools** is reflected in the diagram below.

This chapter began with Fred Trueman's quote: 'Leadership is action not position.' This implies that the word should be treated as a doing word or verb rather than a noun. Leadership is a function and not a role. The following prompts outline the functions that the best leadership fulfils.

Inside out school leadership is:

- **Contextual** because it meets the needs of the school community;
- **Pedagological** because it focuses on learning that leads to achievement;
- **Collegial** because it values everyone and transforms practice through dialogue and teamworking;
- **Emotional** because it seeks to capture the mind and encourages the expression of feelings;

- **Spiritual** because it promotes the sense of a personal journey and mission amongst all those within the school; and
- Always **ethical** because it is based on moral purpose and principle.

Chapter 10

Creating a Vision for Parents as Partners

It is appalling that young people's life chances are still so tied to the fortunes of their parents, and that this situation has not improved over the last three decades.

Sir Peter Lampl (The Sutton Trust)

The Prologue

And Now It's the Other Way Round

The Local Authority had decided to carry out a review to establish why some schools produced high results in reading whilst others seemed to struggle. The evidence clearly suggested that many of the schools in more deprived circumstances still achieved well. I was scheduled to visit one of these schools at the end the week.

The visit started with an interview with the head teacher who also took the role of English subject leader. She was truly passionate but also extremely knowledgeable about this work. She started the conversation with a detailed discussion about the absolute importance of learning to read, but also the complexities of many young children's experiences. The head teacher stressed the importance of meeting the needs of all pupils. Wherever there was a potential barrier to reading she was determined it would be removed. She went on to describe how she had built up a range of reading resources in the form of books, magazines and computer resources. She spoke about the range of intervention programmes the school operated to ensure that identified children received the right support at precisely the right time. The school creatively found funding for the Reading Recovery programme and provided extension work for more able children. One of her essential requirements was that all the adults working with children demonstrated a love of reading and provided high levels of encouragement and support. She had already ensured that this had happened with the teachers and support staff and had recently turned her attention to the parents. This was because she felt they needed to play a more significant role as partners in the educational process.

This was not only a significant piece of work but also a significant challenge. Several parents had relatively low confidence in their ability to carry out appropriate reading activities and provide the right support. Training sessions had been held. Parents had learned how to listen to their child read and had been provided with a range of reading games to play with children. Now, every morning started with a parent and child reading workshop. This was where I was to start my observations.

Soon I was sat opposite a rather large lady and her 6-year-old daughter Amber-Louise. I have a theory that the higher the level of deprivation the more complex the names become. However, the two of them were an absolute delight. The youngster read her work with tremendous expression. She used her knowledge of letters and sounds to decode more complex words and, when this happened, support and praise was offered by the proud and supportive parent. Mum asked appropriate questions to establish how well her child had completed the text and then wrote comments in the child's reading diary before playing a game aimed at developing phonic knowledge.

As the school bell rang Amber-Louise packed her bag, kissed her Mum on the cheek and set off with a spring in her step, and I was left thinking about the positive start she had experienced to the school day.

I returned to my visit notes, got out my clipboard and asked Amber-Louise's Mum if I could ask her a few questions about the school's approach to reading. She spoke with enthusiasm about how the school was working to develop reading skills. In her broad Yorkshire accent she said, 'You see, love, it's like this. Our Amber-Louise used to go to a different school and when she was there she was rubbish at reading but good at writing and now she's come here it's the other way round.' Now that is gushing praise for Yorkshire folk. Just for the record, I met up with Amber-Louise half an hour later when she pulled on my sleeve and read the opening to her story. She was rightly proud of her work.

The school in question recognised the significance in parent partnership. Their school improvement plan always highlighted the next steps the school would take. They also had a parent partnership policy and the chair of governors evaluated its impact on a regular basis. This chapter provides research evidence to show that parental partnership is an absolutely essential part of school improvement and needs to be pursued at all costs. It makes specific reference to how parents and other male role models can help boys in particular to achieve and succeed. The text takes you through the five stages of developing effective parent partnerships:

1. Establishing a free flow of communication
2. Making the best use of parent-volunteers
3. Developing education programmes for parents
4. Encouraging parents to be involved in decision making processes
5. Ensuring all parents are active partners

Finally the chapter helps you to create a vision for further developing parent partnerships in school.

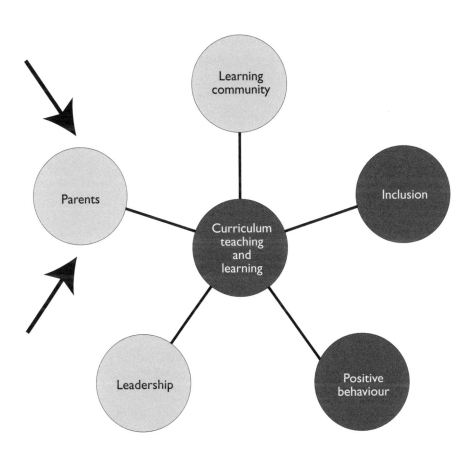

Introduction

> Parental involvement can make the difference between an A* and an also ran. It accounts for one quarter of potential attainment. Its effects are eight times greater than such aspects as social class and parental occupations.
>
> Campaign for Learning

A school is as strong as its weakest link. There is one key aspect of a school's work that is often missed out, and it is the link to parents and the family home. In the drive to constantly raise achievement and standards or the battle to improve the quality of teaching and learning, we fail to remember that in every hour of a child's life only nine minutes are spent in school and fifty-one minutes are spent elsewhere. Teachers are only with the child for fourteen per cent of the time. There are seven key factors that are associated with a child's educational success, most of which lie mainly outside the direct control of schools. The key factors of success are:

- The characteristics of the child as a learner
- The characteristics of the child's family
- The degree of parental involvement
- The effects of the local community
- Peer group pressure
- Family support services
- The quality of the school

All seven of the above points are highly significant in a child's education. However, the attention placed on schools to raise attainment has been immense when they only represent one piece of the jigsaw. School leaders have coped with wave after wave of government initiatives and most have done an exceedingly good job. However, the other issues represent a real challenge and require a change in society's values that cannot be achieved through quick-fix initiatives. However, **inside out leaders** believe that the size of the challenge must not be a reason for avoiding it.

Central government could claim that it has carried out work to ensure the role of parents has become clearer. As early as 1988 governing bodies were required to hold an annual meeting with parents to describe how they had carried out these duties, but these were eventually abandoned due to poor attendance and a lack of interest. There has been further government activity since the creation of the Primary National Strategy in 2003. As a consequence:

- Parent-governor roles have been increased and strengthened.
- The views of parents are more closely analysed in school self-evaluation and within Ofsted inspections.
- More information is required for parents through the school prospectus and the school profile.
- Schools and parents have become compelled to sign home–school agreements.
- There is a requirement on behalf of schools to provide increased information to parents about a school's curriculum and performance.
- There have been several revisions to the way in which school league tables are presented.

Each of these steps may seem admirable and worthwhile; however, they are more about parent power rather than parent partnership. Firstly, the strategies listed add to the current air of compliance and fear that surrounds our schools because they are all about making the school accountable rather than securing a genuine partnership with parents. Secondly, they are not necessarily what the parents want. I accept that parents are increasingly using the above information to select schools for their children. However, many schools regard the home–school agreement as a relatively redundant document and countless schools are unable to fill parent-governor posts because it is not the link parents want with the school. Most parents are less interested in power and more interested in developing partnerships that will help both the school and home to help their children grow up safely and as effective learners. These central government strategies are typical **outside in strategies**; it is now time to consider **inside out strategies**.

Enlightened head teachers have always recognised that both the school and the home are learning environments and that the two need to work together in harmony. **Inside out school leaders** believe that children have two significant educators in their lives—their parents and their teachers. Parents are the prime educators until the child enters the Foundation Stage and remain a major influence on their child's education through school and beyond. In the best schools the roles actually become blurred and there is no clear line to show where the parents' role stops and the teacher's role begins. This is because both have crucial parts to play. However, the impact is always greatest where parents and school work in partnership. There are two obvious strands to this work: parents are fully involved in the life of the school and understand its approaches to teaching, learning and the curriculum; and support is provided for the child at home to provide an element of continuity and to ensure parents can encourage learning.

In 2003, a European Commission survey led by Charles Desforges stressed the importance of the educational capital provided by the home. The review suggested that the nature and the degree of parents' involvement with their child's education may be a greater influence on the child's educational outcomes rather than how good the school is.

> In the primary age, the impact caused by different levels of parental involvement is much bigger than the differences associated with variations in the quality of schools. The scale of the impact is evident across all social classes and ethnic groups.
>
> Charles Desforges, with Alberto Abouchaar, *The Impact of Parental Involvement, Parental Support and Family Education on Pupil Achievement and Adjustment: A Literature Review* (2003)

In short, Desforges is saying that it isn't *who* the parent is, it is what they *do* that counts.

The challenge ahead

The term 'parent' often refers to wide ranging arrangements that adults may have for their children. The past thirty years have seen rapid changes in family structures. The list below produced by the Office for National Statistics shows the complexities of family structures that schools need to work with in establishing appropriate links between schools and homes:

Out of all the dependant children in England and Wales:

- One in four live in single-parent families
- More than one in ten live in stepfamilies
- Two thirds of mothers with dependent children live in stepfamilies (this figure was less than fifty per cent twenty years ago)
- Many children live in families where there are no wage earners

These factors do not lead to parents who are less interested in their children's education; they are simply the complexities within which schools work. Many schools are now offering extended services and hours that help to meet the needs of the modern family. Extended schools can also raise aspirations within a community. This represents considerable progress but it should never be seen as an alternative to developing high quality home–school links.

The opportunities ahead should be limitless. In a highly technological world where ICT is available in both the school and home the opportunities for continuity in learning and parental involvement in learning are significant. Children can potentially extend their learning at home in a fun manner with parental support. Where computers may not be available at home, after school provision is often being made available to pupils and parents. Additionally local libraries can assist. Parents can have access to pupil work folders and a whole range of appropriate school based information. Email contact with parents is increasingly available, although this should never be a replacement for high quality one-to-one discussions about pupil progress or attendance at school events which discuss and demonstrate approaches to teaching and learning or the curriculum.

The role of parents in supporting the education of boys is a particular challenge. The achievement of boys in aspects of literacy is a national concern. In reality, some views held by some parents may run counter to the aims of the school—they may see academic achievement as something that will become more important at secondary school. For example, parents may be more concerned about promoting sporting prowess or allowing boys to develop 'lad'-like qualities. Schools need to be proactive in addressing these issues.

As is stated in an earlier chapter, the magic number is eight. Many writers have commented on the '8:8' culture whereby boys between age 8 and Year 8 start to underachieve. Many of the reasons for this decline relate to issues that exist within society. Colin Noble argues that the issues are environmental rather than developmental and some factors relate to parents.

> Evidence suggests that parents are generally pleased by their children's key stage one results but also relieved that the tests are over for another four years.... Certainly, many parents do not read to their children after their eighth birthday as they did before; even fewer continue to hear their children read. Not only are the SATs a long way off, but there is an assumption that children can now

read and further help is unnecessary. Thus, the large gains made in literacy begin to plateau for many children in year 3.

Colin Noble, 'Helping Boys Do Better in Primary Schools' in Kevin Bleach (ed.) *Raising Boys' Achievement* (2000)

Schools need to raise awareness of these issues with parents. Where the underachievement of boys is a particular issue it should feature in newsletters and other communications sent home to parents, developing campaigns with parents or appointing a governor with responsibility for boys' achievement. In addition, parents need to develop boy-friendly strategies by adding elements of competition or breaking homework into bite-sized chunks. A separate issue is that of male role models; too often boys fail to see fathers and males as effective and active promoters of learning.

The achievement of boys is a serious equal opportunities issue. It is not good enough to simply say that boys get the same experiences as girls. They don't achieve the same outcomes, and parents have a significant role to play in addressing this issue. Whilst seeking high quality support and partnership is a fine ideal, it can be difficult to achieve.

> Differences between parents in their level of involvement are associated with social class, poverty, health and also with parental perceptions about their role and their confidence in fulfilling it. Some parents are put off by feeling put down by teachers.
>
> Charles Desforges, with Alberto Abouchaar, *The Impact of Parental Involvement, Parental Support and Family Education on Pupil Achievement and Adjustment: A Literature Review* (2003)

Research also shows that the better a child is performing in school the more the parents will seek active involvement; where a child is experiencing difficulties parental support will wane. Social class and parental aspiration may well be significant barriers to pupil progress. However, our best schools are not afraid to take on the challenges. The first thing they do is to ensure that they place no barriers in the way and then they work to make parents feel welcomed as genuine partners within the process. **Inside out school leaders** recognise their duty to transform the links between home and school.

> Poor education can be transmitted down the generations. A key influence in a child's educational attainment is the attainment of their parents along with the interest a parent or carer shows in their

child's education. Improving educational outcomes for one generation is a key factor in helping to break this cycle of deprivation.

Department for Work and Pensions, *Opportunities for All. Fourth Annual Report* (2002)

What the best inside out schools do

Inside out schools recognise that there is a five-point progressive scale to developing the best home–school links.

In good schools there is an appropriate free flow of communication between the school and parents

This is due to the high quality work of the named school leader who is responsible and accountable for developing parents as partners. In other words a specific member of staff is responsible for parental links. They ensure that newsletters are parent friendly, free from educational jargon and presented in a style that everybody can read. They are written from a stance of genuine partnership encouraging home and school to work together. They are not used to tell off parents and families or to set a distance between school and home. Where schools have concerns, face-to-face personal contact is far more important. Newsletters should promote a joint air of confidence between school and families and be written wherever possible in a celebratory style. Where it is necessary and possible materials should be translated into home languages. The best schools also make good use of electronic communication.

School reports should contain helpful information about the progress the child has made, their next steps, information about current and future targets and clarify how parents can help in the future. They are not simply a document written by the school. Both the children and parents should have opportunities to contribute. Reports may also contain comments from people other than teachers who have worked with the child. In addition, there are regular meetings between parents and school staff who work with the child. This may not simply be the teacher—it could involve a range of support staff such as teaching assistants or learning mentors and also representatives of other agencies where appropriate.

Early in my headship career, and prior to the advent of the national strategies, I radically reformed the teaching of mathematics within the school. As a consequence the children were doing far more mental arithmetic and open-ended problem solving activities. Our school records were showing that our children were blossoming, making good progress and developing a genuine appetite for mathematics. However, one significant consequence was that there was far less recorded work within the children's exercise books. This made many parents anxious and I was accused of 'bringing in new fangled methods'. I quickly realised my mistake and organised a parents' evening that involved the children to explain what was going on. The parents loved it and became enthusiastic supporters. When significant changes are made to the curriculum it is essential that parents learn what is happening and how they can help. Good schools have a rolling programme of events to inform parents about how different aspects of the curriculum are approached.

Even better schools use a wide range of parent-volunteers

Inside out schools make very good use of parent-volunteers in a whole variety of contexts. It may be through classroom support, help with musical or sporting activities, or asking parents to speak about their areas of expertise. These approaches can seem informal but they offer so much. All the time the parents are in school they are gaining information about the school's approach to teaching and learning. This further equips them to support their own child's learning at home. In recent years this has become a tremendous recruitment technique—many teaching assistants, learning mentors and teachers started life as parent-volunteers.

Many **inside out schools** pay particular attention to engaging with male role models as parent-volunteers. Many boys in our schools do not immediately see males effectively promoting the value of learning. In primary schools where there is a 'laddish' or 'anti-swot' culture where boys believe 'it is cool to be a fool', schools have to actively redress the balance. If this doesn't happen the boys will simply question what our schools are for. In many of our best schools the teacher with responsibility for developing parental involvement actively seeks male role models through newsletters and direct contact. If fathers are unavailable, grandfathers will do just as well. Other schools promote direct links with professional football or rugby clubs or industry.

Many professional football and rugby clubs run their own education programmes and these are often aimed at reluctant boys. One that I am aware of has a learning centre with banks of computers and a range of reading and study materials. Professional sportsmen then work with pupils to develop a range of academic skills. The pupils also have access to some of the sports facilities. In other programmes males from local businesses give time to schools to develop reading skills with boys. Both projects are based on using effective male role models to promote learning.

Even better schools have education programmes for parents

In our next group of schools the leader responsible and accountable for developing links with parents actually recognises that parenting is probably the hardest job in the world. It is far tougher that teaching, politics or being a managing director and therefore extra support, guidance and training is sometimes required. These schools see parents as part of the learning community. They work in subtle ways with parents to build a view within them that they can improve as parents, have a duty to improve as parents and a duty to help improve others. The **inside out school leader** particularly seeks to develop programmes that will help parents to:

- Understand the importance of oracy and develop their child's skill in speaking and listening
- Develop and improve their child's achievement in literacy and numeracy
- Initiate positive behaviour strategies that will help to develop positive attitudes to learning
- Raise their child's self-esteem, confidence and aspiration
- Promote learning as a valued activity that takes place throughout life

Sometimes **inside out schools** will focus on the parents themselves and provide direct training that will improve their:

- Skills within literacy and numeracy
- ICT skills
- Parenting skills
- Knowledge of child development
- Confidence to develop effective links with schools
- Aspirations for self and family

Even better schools involve parents in decision making processes

Now let us be clear about this one. This does not necessarily mean the parents always make the decisions. It may be that they have the full knowledge of a situation and understand why a decision has been taken. At a whole school level our best schools:

- Know what parents think about the school because they seek ways of asking them
- Tell parents what is important to the school and its staff
- Find ways of getting parents to contribute towards the school vision and when it is completed find ways of disseminating and articulating the vision to parents
- Negotiate with parents around sensitive issues such as a move from single-aged to mixed-age classes
- Tell parents about the curriculum and particularly proposed changes to the curriculum
- Involve parents in the creation of key policies
- Respond to any parental concerns relating to the curriculum

The challenge is, of course, to select the correct methodology. Schools are increasingly canvassing the views of parents through interviews and questionnaires and taking heed of the comments made. Other schools organise informal drop-in sessions. Head teachers are increasingly found at the school gates gaining the opinions of parents. Many schools have longstanding parents' associations which are used to disseminate information and formulate future school policy. Some schools are increasingly using the flexibility of modern technologies to involve parents in shaping the future direction of the school.

However, there is another key element to involving parents in decision making activities and that relates to the individual child. Too many parents complain that they feel helpless when key decisions are made about their own child. Parents know their children best and they will want to contribute to their child's education rather than simply be told about it. Every parent deserves:

- Genuine dialogue about their child's achievements and what they need to do next. This dialogue must be a two-way process and not just the school 'telling' the parent.

- These meetings should take place within a clear framework where everyone is clear about the role and the purpose of the meeting.
- All information presented should be in an accessible form and based on clear evidence.
- The school and parents (and the child) will be clear on any targets that have been set and each other's duty in achieving the target.

There are certain sensitive times when schools must be particularly clear with information and ensure that full parental discussion takes place. These occasions include:

- Possible exclusion
- Poor behaviour
- Truancy
- Poor attendance
- Bullying
- Lack of concentration
- Lack of home support
- Lack of parental aspiration and expectation

The best schools ensure that all parents are engaged as full and active partners in their child's education

The best schools involve parents and carers as one of their specific aims. Senior leaders and managers promote parent involvement vigorously and everyone in the school is totally committed to it and seeks to make parents and carers full and active partners. They do this by identifying exactly how parents can help children as learners and set up appropriate strategies which are constantly evaluated and revised until they have maximum impact. These strategies include:

- Giving parents regular and easily accessible information about their child's current programme of work, the school's approaches to teaching and learning across the curriculum, and providing precise guidance on how parents can help at home.
- Running workshop sessions in certain key areas of the curriculum, especially reading, writing, mathematics and information and communication technology.
- Holding periodic surgeries to support specific areas of learning.
- Ensuring parent learning is recognised as a high profile activity across the school.

- Developing a parents as partners website which provides additional information as well as links to other key parental websites.
- Organising events either in school or through homework where parents and children undertake learning activities together.

I recently visited a school where outside every classroom was a large picture of a tree. Each week different leaves were added, and written on each leaf were the key areas of study that were going to be taught over the next week. There were also tips on how parents could help at home. The parents were always welcome to discuss this further with the class teacher.

Creating a vision for parent partnership

Parents have for too long been the missing link in the process of improving pupil progress and helping schools to provide pupils with essential life skills. The following reality check should be used by school leadership teams to provide high quality dialogue about the issues raised. It will help you to create a vision for your school that creates strong and powerful relationships with parents that will help them to become genuine partners in their child's education in three years' time. After that has been completed the challenge is to identify what will be different in one year's time.

Parents as partners: a reality check	Actions required
Our school believes that children's future prospects are dependent on the school, the child and the family working as partners	*need more*
Our school has a rigorously enforced parental involvement policy	✓
We can demonstrate how we enhance parental links year by year	✓
Improving parental partnership is always a key element in the annual school improvement plan	✓
A member of the school leadership team is empowered and accountable for the current quality and further developments of parental links	✓ *ony*

Parents as partners: a reality check	Actions required
Our school offers opportunities for parents to take up learning	✓
The school makes all parents and families welcome and works hard to build and maintain strong relationships with parents	needs to develop
Our school does as much as it reasonably can to encourage the involvement of all parents in their children's learning both at school and at home	✓
Our school provides parents with opportunities to have a genuine say in and be an active part of the life and work of the school	needs to develop
Our school is sensitive towards and supportive of the varying backgrounds, needs and circumstances of all pupils and their families	✓
Our school has procedures to ask parents what they think about the school	✓ evidence trails
Our school is an integral part of the local community	needs to develop
Our parents understand our school aim and vision statements and help us to fulfil them	✓✓
Our parents have appropriate information about the school curriculum and are always fully informed of major innovations	✓✓
We allocate parents a minimum of ten minutes per term with teachers	✓

 Now describe your vision of how parents will become genuine partners in their children's education.

 Now state what will be different in one year's time.

Summary

For the last nine years I have worked in a Local Authority's School Improvement Service. I am trying to keep quiet about it because I may not represent good value for money. Research by Sacker, Schoon and Bartley (2002) would indicate that if you took an average attaining primary school and introduced a team of Local Authority improvement officers the school would improve by around five per cent across a range of measures for 7 year olds. If, however, the school focused on making their parents as good as the best parents nationally the growth would be twenty-nine per cent. Schools must rise to this challenge because:

> It is appalling that young people's life chances are still so tied to the fortunes of their parents, and that this situation has not improved over the last three decades.
>
> Sir Peter Lampl (The Sutton Trust)

Chapter 11

Putting the Pieces Together

Vision without action is daydreaming.
Action without vision is a nightmare.

Japanese proverb

'But I have no desire for Ofsted to name my school as an outstanding school. I just want to do the right things.' This statement is regularly put to me as I conclude work relating to vision. This is because I know that if schools have a true vision based on providing a high quality education, personalised to the needs of the community, there is every chance of them receiving a highly successful inspection. I always make two responses when I hear this statement:

- Firstly, there is nothing wrong with having the aspiration, ambition and desire to be outstanding. This is the extrinsic reward.
- Secondly, if you use the materials in this book to create a vision for the future, and then follow your plans with rigour, you will be doing the right things for your pupils. This is the intrinsic reward. The positive inspection judgement will just follow and it should be celebrated.

The systems described in the book work for two reasons. Firstly, the chapters are based on the key improvement drivers of:

- Teaching and learning and the curriculum
- Developing positive behaviour and attitudes and emotional intelligence in pupils
- Pupil inclusion
- Creating a high quality professional learning community
- Improving school leadership
- Engaging parents as partners

If the guidance in this book is fully followed you will also meet the five outcomes of the Every Child Matters agenda, which are that children will be:

- Safe
- Healthy
- Enjoy and achieve
- Economically aware
- Positive contributors to society

Secondly, the systems in this book work because they combine the skills of four wonderfully committed and totally fictitious head teachers. Each of them prefers to think using a different part of the brain. Now that you have come to the end of the book I will introduce them to you.

Our first head teacher is truly a visionary woman. She has the capacity to see a world in the future where all classrooms are stimulating places and children are absorbed in rich and vivid tasks. The pupils are highly motivated and well-behaved. Sadly, though, she is a dreamer who cannot plan out the steps to achieve her vision. Her hobbies could include photography, art and walking.

Meet the school leader who can dream it for the children

She is:
- Imaginative
- Visionary
- Sees the big picture
- Artistic
- A conceptualiser
- Seeks awe and wonder

However she is less skilled at:
- Articulating and disseminating vision by developing and delivering strategic plans
- Monitoring and evaluation
- Developing leadership structures
- Day-to-day management

Our second head teacher is a very good verbal communicator. Talk is all important to her—she sees it as an essential tool to provide clarity. She cares deeply about everybody in the school community and cares deeply about their well-being. As a consequence her days can be full of dialogue, conversations and meetings. However, she spends so much time on this that sometimes very little action takes place. Her hobbies include music.

Meet the school teacher who energises it through the adults using high quality communication skills

Her positive attributes are:
- Interpersonal skills
- Emotional intelligence
- Seeks spiritual intelligence
- Values the spoken word
- Values staff well-being
- Musical

However she is less skilled at:
- Developing long-term vision
- Monitoring and evaluation
- Developing and delivering strategic plans
- Day-to-day management

Organisation is the key feature of our third head teacher. Every staff meeting is listed for the full year. Policies are all written, colour coded and filed away. Every box is ticked because all tasks are completed to schedule. There is a clear air of control within the school. Sadly, overall, the school is rather a dull place. She runs her school in the same style as Mr Stimpson the hapless head teacher played by John Cleese in the film *Clockwise*. Many might regard her as a control freak.

Meet the school leader who drives it through developing the key processes and systems

Her positive attributes are:
- She is controlled and controls
- Conservative
- Plans meticulously
- Organisational skills
- Administrative skills
- Systematic
- Tidy

She is less skilled at:
- Developing long-term vision
- Verbal communication skills
- Seeking imaginative solutions
- Evaluation

Our fourth and final head teacher is an expert at analysing the school data. He loves the day when he receives his electronic interactive Panda. He can set targets to Fischer Family Trust D predictions with frightening accuracy. He can tell you about the attainment of each and every sub-group of pupils including left-handed boys wearing blue trainers. Sadly he could be so engrossed in the data he may not always see a clear route to improvement.

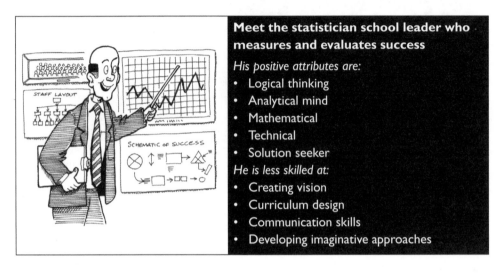

Meet the statistician school leader who measures and evaluates success

His positive attributes are:
- Logical thinking
- Analytical mind
- Mathematical
- Technical
- Solution seeker

He is less skilled at:
- Creating vision
- Curriculum design
- Communication skills
- Developing imaginative approaches

I'm sure you'll recognise personal traits in all four of these headteachers. Part of your challenge as a head is how you bring the best elements of all of them together to get the best out of yourself, your staff and your school.

By following the materials in this book you will now be in a position to finalise a vision statement for how your school will look in three years' time. By taking all the plans you have noted in Chapters 4, 5, 6 and 7 you will be in a position to create a vision for your work with pupils. By taking all the plans you have noted in Chapters 8, 9 and 10 you will be ready to write a vision statement for your work with adults. However, you must remember that this is only half of the process. 'Stage 3: Drive it through key systems and processes' (page 30) described the need to devise the right systems and processes that will drive your dream into reality—this is the third sector of your vision. After that you must create the final part of the vision which is to establish the key targets and measures of success that you will establish to know that you are being successful. Guidance on this can be found in 'Stage 4: Measure it through the things you value' (page 32). This is the fourth sector of your vision.

But don't forget there was one final challenge. Once the vision statement has been written and prepared, and even after it has been supported by a small number of high quality policies and documents, it is not yet complete. Your new vision statement can too easily become very forgettable. It doesn't matter how good the documentation, in a fast moving world it can slip from the forefront of your thinking. There is also the highly dangerous fidelity factor which soon seeps into the system. As a consequence, the school starts to get pulled back to old ways of working. This prevents planned systematic change from becoming embedded. The challenge is therefore to get the vision statement and key policies down to one emblem, logo or motto which is high profile within the school and that is understood by staff, pupils and parents. Information about this is available on page 34. However, there is a final quotation from a school's vision statement to leave with you:

> Enter, our doors are open to all,
> Please come in, and wander through my rooms
> Fill up your senses on your visit,
> Touch my solid walls where firm foundations are building strong
>   skilful citizens
> Listen to the healthy hubbub of vibrant learning, bubbling through
>   my being.
> Feel my soft blanket of security nurturing my learners enabling
>   them to fly.
> Our vision is sharp.
> Come in and you will see
> Premier league learners in action accepting the true challenges of
>   the future.

As you create your vision for a new and wonderful future, and become a genuine **inside out school**, I wish you every success and remember:

> Vision without action is daydreaming. Action without vision is a nightmare.

Bibliography

Alexander, R. J. (2000) *Culture and Pedagogy: International Comparisons in Primary Education* (Oxford: Blackwell).

Arrowsmith, R. (2001) 'A Right Performance' in D. Gleeson and C. Husbands (eds), *The Performing School* (London: RoutledgeFalmer).

Arthur, J., Grainger, T. and Wray, D. (eds) (2006) *Learning to Teach in the Primary School* (London: Routledge).

Aspinwall, K. (1988) *Leading the Learning School* (London: Lemos and Crane).

Beetlestone, F. (1988 [1980]) *Creative Children, Imaginative Teaching* (London: Open University Press).

Bennis, W. (1989) *On Becoming a Leader* (Reading, MA: Addison-Wesley).

—— and Nanus, B. (1997) *Leaders: Strategies for Taking Charge* (New York: Harper Collins).

Blake, R. R. and Mouton, J. S. (1978) *The New Managerial Grid* (Maidenhead: McGraw Hill).

Blanden, J. and Machin. S. (2007) *Recent Changes in Intergenerational Mobility in Britain* (funded by the Sutton Trust) (London School of Economics and the University of Surrey).

Bleach, K. (2000) *Raising Boys' Achievement in Schools* (Wiltshire: Trentham Books).

Board of Education (1937) *Handbook of Suggestions for Teachers* (London: HMSO).

—— (1959) *Primary Education* (London: HMSO).

Boston Consultancy Group (2007) *A Report on the Returns to Investments in Educational Programmes* (for the Sutton Trust) (<http://www.suttontrust.uk>).

Bryant, K. (2003) *Creative Use of Data: Measuring What We Value*, Burning Issues in Primary Education 8 (Birmingham: National Primary Trust).

Carroll, L. (2003 [1865]) *Alice's Adventures in Wonderland* (London: Penguin Classics).

Ciulla, J. (1998) *The Heart of Leadership* (Westport, CT: Praeger Publishers).

—— (1998) *The Working Life: The Promise and Betrayal of Modern Work* (New York: Random House).

Conger, J. A. (1992) *Learning to Lead* (San Francisco: Jossey-Bass).

Curran, A. (2006) 'How the Brain Works' in Ian Gilbert et al., *The Big Book of Independent Thinking* (Carmarthen, Crown House).

Cuttance, P. (1998) 'Quality Assurance Reviews as a Catalyst for School Improvement in Australia', in A. Hargreaves, A. Lieberman, M. Fullan and D. Hopkins (eds), *The International Handbook of Educational Change* (Dordrecht: Kluwer Academic Publishers).

Department for Education and Skills (DfES) (1999) *All Our Futures: Creativity, Culture and Education* (London: DfES).

—— (2003) *Excellence and Enjoyment: A Strategy for Primary Schools* (London: DfES).

Department for Work and Pensions (DWP) (2002) *Opportunity for All. Fourth Annual Report 2002* (London: DWP).

Department of Health (2005) *National Service Framework for Mental Health—Five Years On* (London: Department of Health).

Desforges, C., with Abouchaar, A. (2003) *The Impact of Parental Involvement, Parental Support and Family Education on Pupil Achievement and Adjustment: A Literature Review*, Research Report No. 433 (London: DfES).

Donelly, J. H., Ivancevich, J. M. and Gibson, J. L. (2005) *Organizations: Behavior, Structure, Processes*, 5th edn (Plano, TX: Business Publications).

Elton, Lord (1989) *Discipline in Schools: Report of the Committee of Enquiry Chaired by Lord Elton* (London: HMSO).

Fullan, M. (1993) *Changing Forces: Probing the Depths of Educational Reform* (London: Falmer Press).

Gallwey, W. T. (1975) *The Inner Game of Tennis* (London: Pan MacMillan).

Gardner, H. (1984) *Frames of Mind: The Theory of Multiple Intelligence* (London: Fontana).

Gatto, J. T. (2005) *Dumbing Us Down: The Hidden Curriculum of Compulsory Education* (British Columbia: New Society Publishers).

Gilbert, I., et al. (2006) *The Big Book of Independent Thinking* (Carmarthen: Crown House).

Gleeson, D. and Husbands, C. (2001) (eds) *The Performing School* (London: RoutledgeFalmer).

Goleman, D. (1997) *Emotional Intelligence* (London: Bloomsbury).

Handy, C. R. (1982) *Understanding Organisations* (London: Penguin Business).

Hoffman, E. (2002) *For You, Dear Teacher* (Middlewich: Learn to Learn).

Hollander, E. P. (1978) *Leadership Dynamics* (New York: Free Press).

Hurley, C. (1997) *Could Do Better: School Reports of the Great and Good* (London: Simon and Schuster).

Jones, D., Raby. M., Tolfree, T. and Gross, J. (2006) *The Long Term Costs of Literacy Difficulties* (KPMG Foundation).

Leighton, R. (2004) *Primary Practice* (Birmingham: National Primary Trust).

McGuiness, C. (1999) *From Thinking Skills to Thinking Classrooms: A Review and Evaluation of Approaches for Developing Pupils' Thinking*. Research Report RR115 (London: DfEE).

Mahony, T. (2004) *Principled Leadership* (Carmarthen: Crown House).

Middlewood, D., Parker, R. and Beere, J. (2005) *Creating a Learning School* (London: Paul Chapman).

Ministry of Education (1959) *Primary Education* (London: HMSO).

National College for School Leadership (2004) *Learning Centred Leadership* (Nottingham: NCSL).

Bibliography

Noble, C. (2000) 'Helping Boys Do Better in Primary Schools' in K. Bleach (ed.) *Raising Boys' Achievement* (Stoke on Trent: Trentham Books).

Northouse, P. G. (2004) *Leadership Theory and Practice* (London: Sage).

Office for Standards in Education (Ofsted) (2001) *Continuing Professional Development for Teachers* (<http://www.ofsted.go.uk>).

Pinker, S. (1999) *How the Brain Works* (London and New York, Penguin).

Qualification and Curriculum Authority (QCA) (2003) *Creativity: Find It, Promote It* (<http://www.qca.org.uk>).

Sacker, A., Schoon, I. and Bartley, M. (2002) 'Social Inequality in Educational Achievement and Psychological Adjustment throughout Childhood: Magnitude and Mechanisms', *Social Science and Medicine* 55: 863–880.

Smith, A. (2000) *Accelerated Learning in Practice* (London: Network Education).

Southworth, G. (2004) 'How Leaders Influence What Happens in Classrooms' in National College for School Leadership, *Learning Centred Leadership* (Nottingham: NCSL).

Stodgill, R. (1974) *Handbook of Leadership: A Survey of Theory and Research* (New York: Free Press).

Stoll, L. (1999) 'Realising Our Potential: Understanding and Developing Capacity for Lasting Improvement', *School Improvement and School Effectiveness* 10, 4: 503–532.

——, Fink, D. and Earl, L. (2003) *It's About Learning (and It's About Time)* (London: RoutledgeFalmer).

Trueman, F. S. (2005) *As it Was: The Memoirs* (London: Pan).

Unicef (2007) *Child Poverty in Perspective: An Overview of Child Well-being in Rich Countries* (Florence: Innocenti Research Centre).

Wyse, D. (2006) 'Approaches to the Curriculum', in J. Arthur, T. Grainger and D. Wray (eds), *Learning to Teach in the Primary School* (London: RoutledgeFalmer).

Young, J. Z. (1987) *Philosophy and the Brain* (Oxford: Oxford University Press).

Index

Leadership with a Moral Purpose

Independent Thinking Ltd was set up in 1993 to 'Enrich children's lives by changing the way they think - and so to change the world'. Since that time this unique organisation, led by its founder Ian Gilbert, has worked across the UK and around the world with young people, teachers, school leaders, advisors, governors and parents and in all sectors of education, to include:

- INSET
- Conferences
- Student Events
- Consultancy
- Books
- Podcasts

- Videocasts
- Learning Tools
- TV and Radio Broadcasts
- Articles
- Learning Technologies

To find out more and to access a wide range of free resources please check out www.independentthinking.co.uk.

The Independent Thinking Series of books is the latest in a line of innovative resources to help teachers and schools address the many challenges of the 21st century:

The Big Book of Independent Thinking: *Do things no one does or do things everyone does in a way no one does* — Edited by Ian Gilbert
A 'bible' for teachers with ideas and inspiration from many of our Associates across a wide range of topics. — ISBN 978-190442438-3

Little Owl's Book of Thinking: *An Introduction to Thinking Skills* — Ian Gilbert
An introduction to thinking, learning and living for younger children. — ISBN 978-190442435-2

The Little Book of Thunks: *260 questions to make your brain go ouch!* — Ian Gilbert
Contagious philosophical questions to get young people's brains to hurt. — ISBN 978-184590062-5

The Buzz: *A practical confidence builder for teenagers* — David Hodgson
Strategies for helping young people know themselves better for improved motivation, communication and success in school and beyond. — ISBN 978-190442481-9

The Learner's Toolkit: *Developing Emotional Intelligence, Instilling Values for Life, Creating Independent Learners and Supporting the SEAL Framework for Secondary Schools* — Jackie Beere Edited by Ian Gilbert
Every teacher's essential guide to creating truly independent learners, confident and resilient in their ability to learn and learn well. — ISBN 978-184590070-0

www.independentthinking.co.uk   www.crownhouse.co.uk

Essential Motivation in the Classroom
An entertaining and inspiring read full of useful, practical advice on how to motivate children and how children can learn to motivate themselves. — ISBN 978-041526619-2

The Little Book of Big Stuff about the Brain: *The true story of your amazing brain* — Andrew Curran Edited by Ian Gilbert
The brain has never been easier to comprehend. With the help of Andrew Curran's witty prose and illustrations, you will come to understand how the brain works and the implications this has for learning. — ISBN 978-184590085-4

The Little Book of Music for the Classroom — Nina Jackson Edited by Ian Gilbert
Simply and effectively teaches you what music to use, when and why. Put away your whale song CD and your James Last box set and explore how music really can transform your classroom.
— ISBN 978-184590091-5

Are You Dropping the Baton? *From effective collaboration to all-through schools – your guide to improving transition* — David Harris Edited by Ian Gilbert
Tackles transition head on, provides countless examples of how primary and secondary schools can work together more effectively.
— ISBN 978-184590081-6

www.independentthinking.co.uk   www.crownhouse.co.uk